Introducing Batik

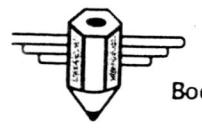

Introducing Batik

Evelyn Samuel

B T Batsford Limited London
Watson-Guptill Publications New York

First published 1968
Reprinted 1971
Third Impression 1973
Library of Congress Catalog Card Number 68-16174

ISBN 0 7134 2402 8

Made and Printed in Great Britain by
William Clowes & Sons Limited Beccles Suffolk
For the Publishers
B T Batsford Limited
4 Fitzhardinge Street London W1 and
Watson-Guptill Publications
One Astor Plaza New York NY 10036

Contents

Acknowledgment

I acknowledge with grateful thanks the following who have helped so much in the preparation of this book:

William Palmer, MA, FLC, Head of the Department of Biological Sciences, Homerton College, Cambridge for his skill and patience in taking the photographs, with the exception 12, 18, 41, 53, 57, 68 and 73 taken by Ramsay and Muspratt, Cambridge, and 43 and 44 taken by Dennis Mynott. Nora Proud, Senior Lecturer, Art Department, Whitelands College of Education, Putney for her generous advice and encouragement. The Head Mistress and girls of the Manor School, Cambridge, for illustrations 13, 20, 24, 27, 29, 30, 31, 32, 33, 34, 35, 37, 46–50, 54, and 72. Jenny Cox and pupils of the Village College, Swavesey, for illustrations 43–5 and 51. Christine Chilton for 52, 68 and 69 and for her helpful criticism; Sheila Jackson for 60; Margaret Mayne for 42; Pamela Norman for 64 and 65; Felicity Norman for 21 and 22; Kathleen Sandback for 61, 62 and 76; Catherine Cobb, Christine Mitchell and Deryn O'Connor who provided information, and loan of Malayan fabrics and tools. Thelma M. Nye, Craft Editor of B. T. Batsford Limited for her helpful suggestions and guidance. Madeline Wright for clerical assistance and my father for his practical help at all times.

E.S.   Cambridge 1968

Introduction

Batik is an Indonesian word which describes a form of resist printing obtained when hot wax, an effective resist to dye, is applied to the fabric. Fine patterns are often made by using a tjanting, which is a tool for applying hot wax (1). Sometimes wax patterns from Indonesia are printed on the cloth using a tjap, the name given to a metal block made, in intricate lattice work, of strips of metal with fine metal rods attached to give a variety of patterns (2, 3, 4). The block is dipped into a shallow tray of hot wax. When removed, the surplus wax is shaken off and the block pressed heavily on the fabric, and thumped hard.

When the fabric is dyed, only the unwaxed areas of the cloth take the colour. Dyeing is carried out in cool water to prevent the wax from melting. Nowadays a variety of primitive cold water dyes are available. These are useful for experimental purposes and to gain a working knowledge of dyes suitable for this craft.

Although batik as a craft is practised mainly in Java and Indonesia, resist printing and dyeing with wax is also known in South East India, Europe and parts of Africa. In recent years batik and related techniques have become popular with craftsmen, teachers and young school children in Britain and America.

2 A tjap seen from below

3 A tjap seen from above

4 Print made from the tjap on cloth, then dyed

5 Detail of border of cotton scarf from Malaya

6 Detail of bird design showing use of
tjap and tjanting

7 Detail of sarong border and flower design

8, 9 Details of recent Javanese batik

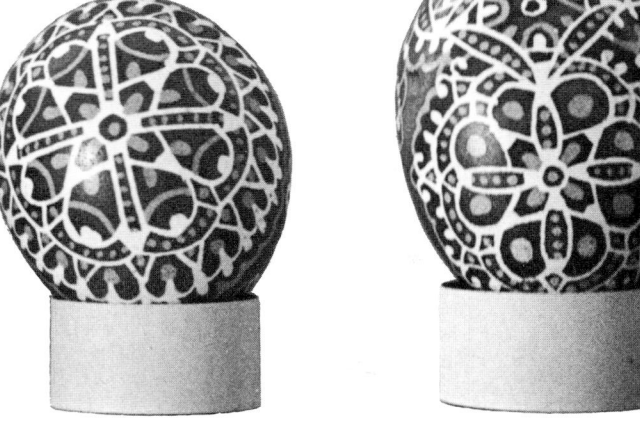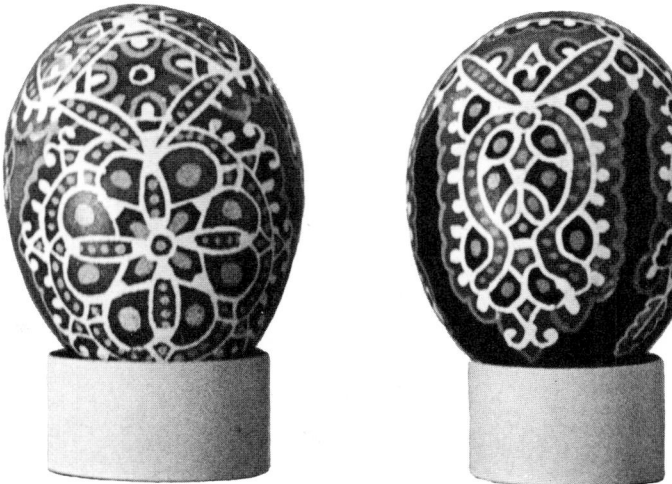

10 Easter eggs from mid-Europe, using traditional wax patterns made with pin heads and wax pens

13

Basic Equipment

For waxing

An electric heater, gas ring or hotplate, standing on a sheet of asbestos or other fireproof material
A double boiler, or saucepan in which are placed a number of tin containers
A flat table surface covered with newspaper
Candles or blocks of paraffin wax
Night-lights or calorettes (similar to night-lights only giving more heat)
Resin or beeswax obtained from hardware stores
Tjanting: brushes; blocks; and stampers for making patterns
A wooden frame on which to pin the cloth.

When a number of children are working at the same time, tins of various sizes are needed both to hold the wax and to make individual heaters. These heaters are made by punching holes and putting in lighted calorettes to keep the wax warm when placed in the tin container on top of the improvised heater.

For dyeing

A plastic or enamel bowl or bath (not metal)
A plastic or glass measure
Rubber gloves
Polythene sheeting
Newspaper to cover the working surface
Plastic spoons of various sizes
Small bowls or jars in which to mix dyes.

Preparation of the fabric for waxing

Fabrics used for dyeing and printing must be washed thoroughly to remove all traces of dressings, sizes, and natural oils. Best results are obtained on cotton, cotton lawn, calico, silk and linen, also mixtures of wool and cotton. Materials with special finishes, such as crease resistant, non-iron, or drip dry are not suitable for beginners as the dyes do not penetrate these surfaces easily. When the material is ironed free from creases, it is ready for the application of wax resist.

11 Equipment for waxing, standing on asbestos square

Method of heating wax

A simple way of obtaining wax is by melting candles or pieces cut from a block of paraffin wax. These are melted in a tin which rests in a saucepan of boiling water over an electric hotplate or gas ring. Small coffee tins or similar containers are very useful for this. Several tins can be fitted into one saucepan and the wax melted and then distributed to the various groups in the class. The groups keep their wax hot over burning night-lights in small coffee tins with many holes punches in the sides, especially around the top rim to allow the air to pass in and out. This is important as otherwise the lights go out.

The tins containing wax are returned to the boiling water in the saucepan for re-heating from time to time. It is useful to have a reserve of hot wax ready to pour into any tins that come back empty.

By adding a small quantity of resin or beeswax to the wax and melting them together, a tougher and less brittle wax is obtained. A useful quantity is 1 part resin or beeswax to 4 parts paraffin wax. It should be emphasised that when handling the hot wax great care must be taken at all times to prevent accidents, especially where children are concerned.

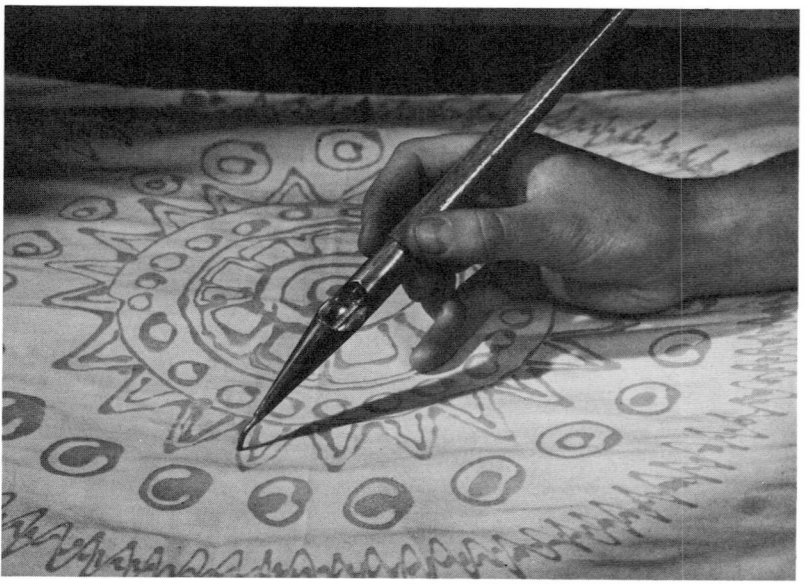
12 Close up of tjanting

Application of the wax

The material to be waxed is spread out on the layers of newspaper which cover the working surface. If possible, the material should be pinned across a frame (an old picture frame will do); the wax will then pass through the material but not adhere to the paper beneath, thus preventing cracking or damage to the wax which can be caused by peeling off the paper.

The hot wax can be applied in many ways.

Tjanting

The tjanting produces fine lines, dots, circles and a variety of surface textures. The tool is dipped into hot wax to fill the reservoir, then carried to the surface of the cloth. To prevent the wax from dripping on the work, hold a piece of paper under the spout and carry it over the cloth to the working point. The small tube discharges a thin trail of wax, varying according to the thickness of the tube and the heat of the wax. If the wax is hot enough, a trail of fine transparent lines is left behind.

1

2

3

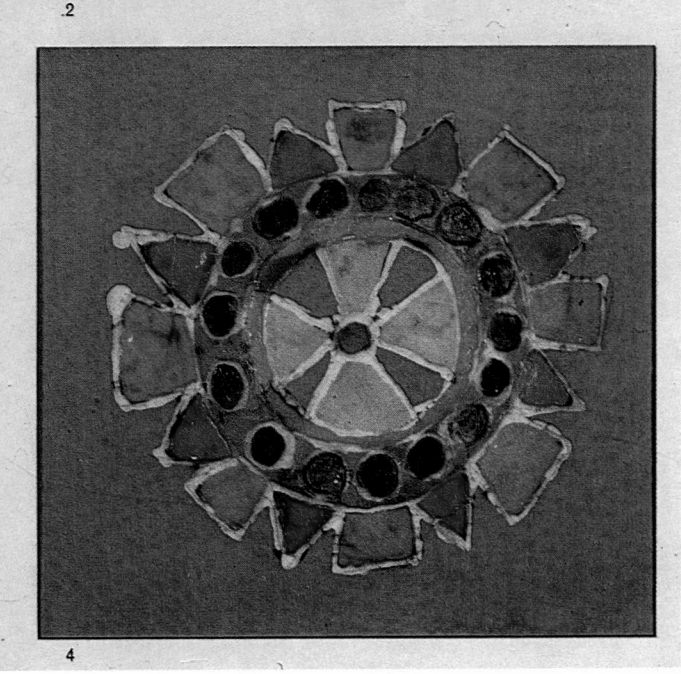

4

5

6

Painting a waxed design
1 Design waxed on cloth
2 Areas painted with dye
3 Painted areas waxed over
4 Cloth dipped in background area
5 Wax boiled off
   This could be the final stage but the
sample was taken one stage further
6 After process No 4 the background
   was waxed all over and crumpled,
   and dyed in Brentamine Fast Black
   K Salt, and dried
7 Wax boiled off, and cloth washed
   and ironed

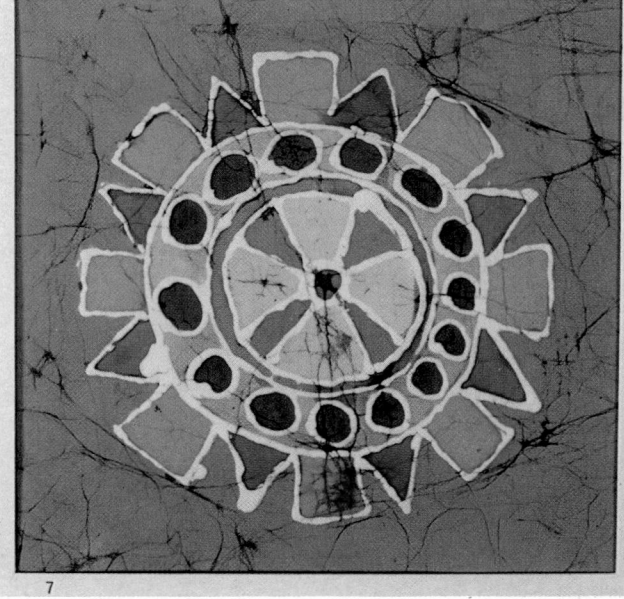

7

13 Painting on wax with a brush

14 Dots and stripes using a paint brush only

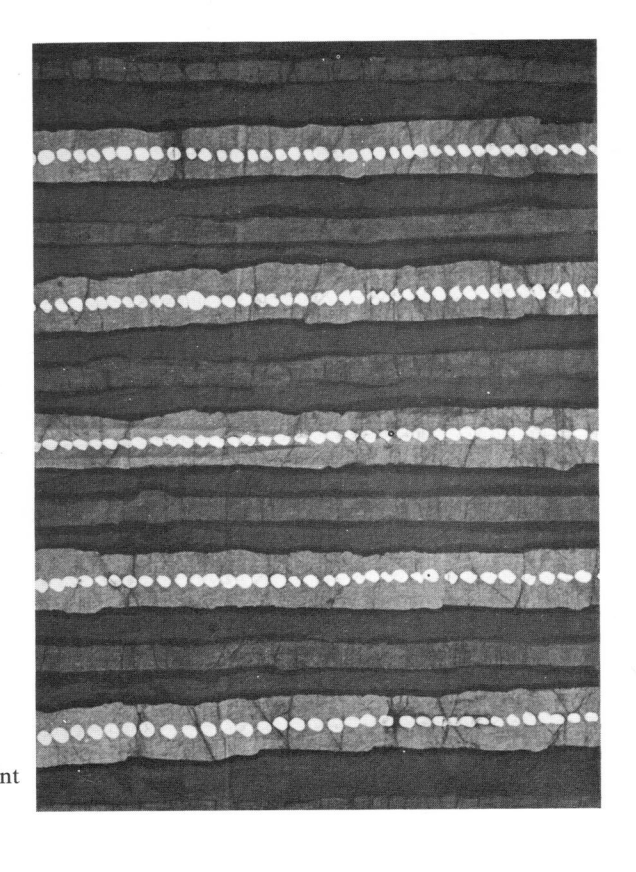

Brushes

Ordinary paint brushes and flat brushes are used to fill in large areas or to make stripes and squares, or to make spots by using the tip only.

Blocks

Blocks made from metal rods, pins stuck in corks, knitting-needle knobs, wooden blocks, nails, bolts and nuts, felt shapes on wood and cardboard rolls, can all produce interesting patterns when dipped into hot wax and then pressed on to the surface of the cloth. For this type of block it is easier if the wax is melted into tin lids or shallow baking tins.

If paraffin wax is accidentally dripped on to the material it can be removed with a drop of paraffin rubbed on the spot after the wax has been scratched off.

15 Variety of stamps and blocks suitable for printing

16 Prints made from the blocks. The hexagonal one is made with a large metal nut from a bolt, with a piece of wood stuck in the hole. The round spot is a nail head and the triangle and oblong, a piece of carpet underlay glued on a piece of wood. The large circle is made by using a cardboard cylinder

17 This pattern was made by printing on the cloth with a block made from pins in a cork. The fabric was then dyed blue. Next, the spots were printed on the blue, in wax, the first circle waxed with a brush and this time dyed in yellow changing the unwaxed area to green. Finally these circles were waxed, and the whole piece dipped in Procion navy dye

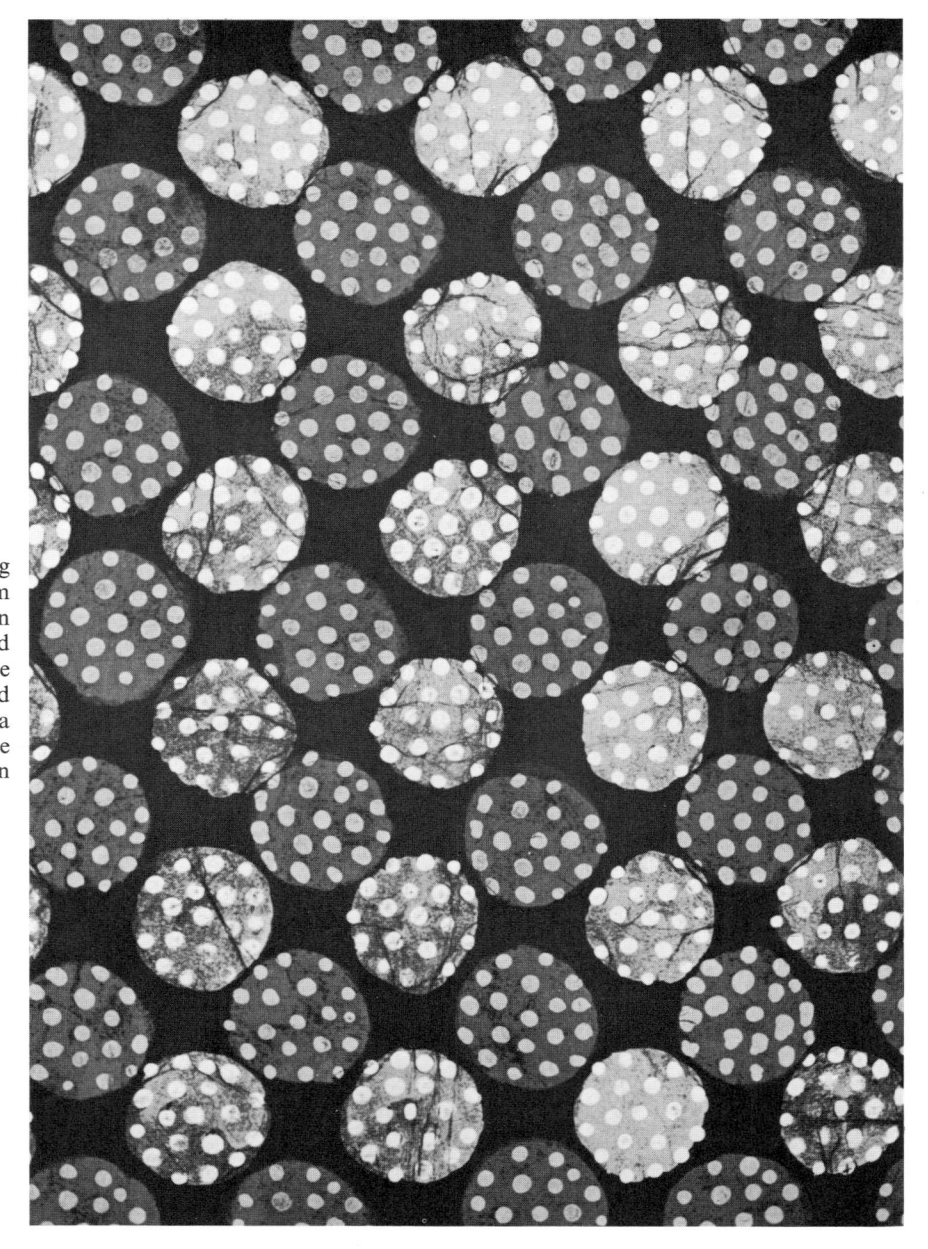

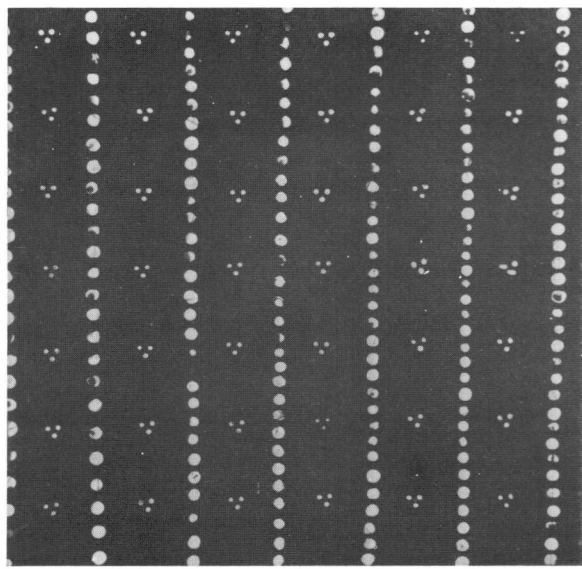

18 Pattern made with tip of brush and three glass-headed pins pushed into a cork. The cloth was dyed in an indigo vat

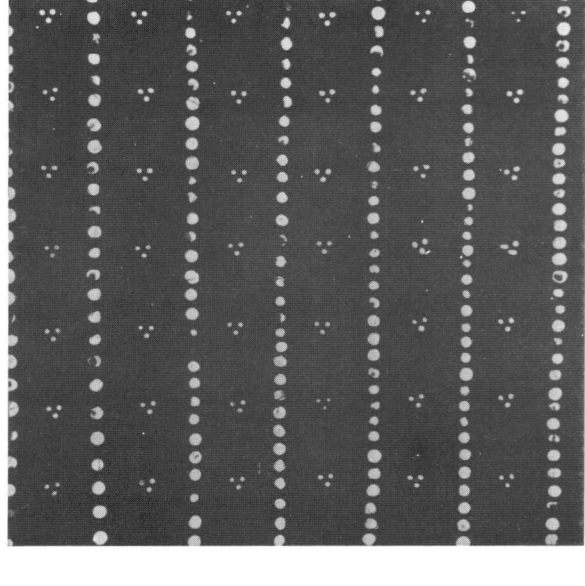

19 Patterns made with pins and strips of wood. Stripes and patterns of wax made with tjanting and dyed in potassium permanganate solution

20 A dragon made by a 12-year-old girl. Wax was dripped from a candle on to paper and brushed with melted wax. It was then painted with coloured inks, and the process repeated when the ink was dry

Candle drips

Other patterns and textures are made if wax is dripped directly on to the material from the candle or night-light.

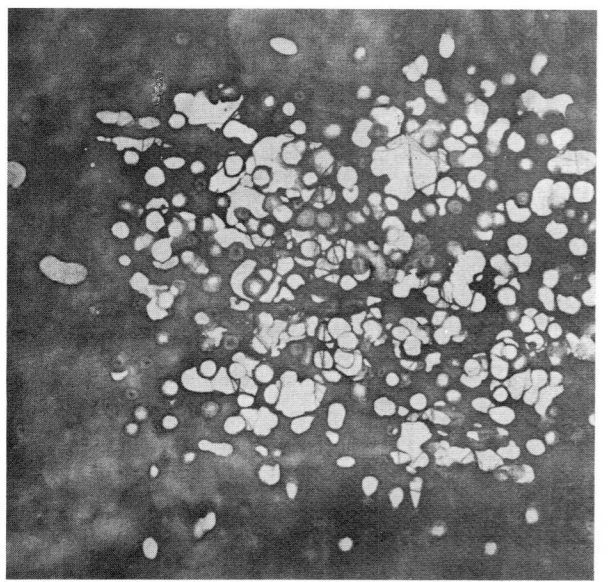

21 Wax from a candle dripped freely on cloth by an 8-year-old, then the cloth was dyed

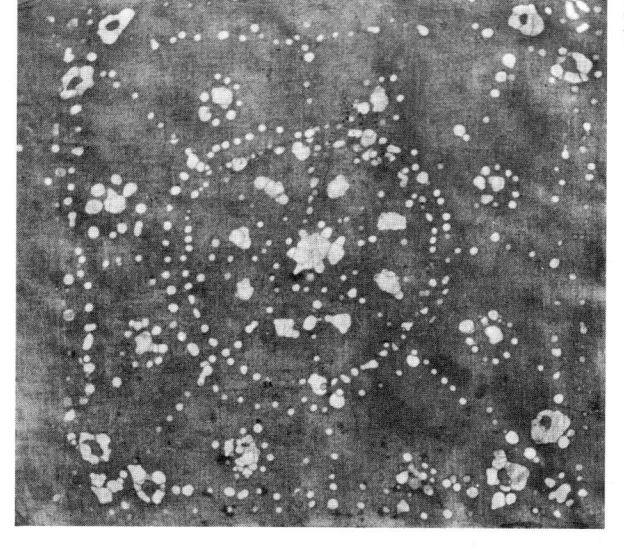

22 Wax was dripped in a definite pattern by this 8-year-old

23 Patterns made by rubbing different
objects with a candle

24 A collage made of patterns drawn
on paper with the side of a candle then
brushed with coloured ink. An exer-
cise to explore the possibility of wax-
resist patterns

Candle wax rubbing

Interesting resist patterns are made if the fabric is stretched over
various textures, such as wire mesh, metal baskets, bricks and other
surfaces found in the room or school, and rubbed with a candle or wax
crayon.

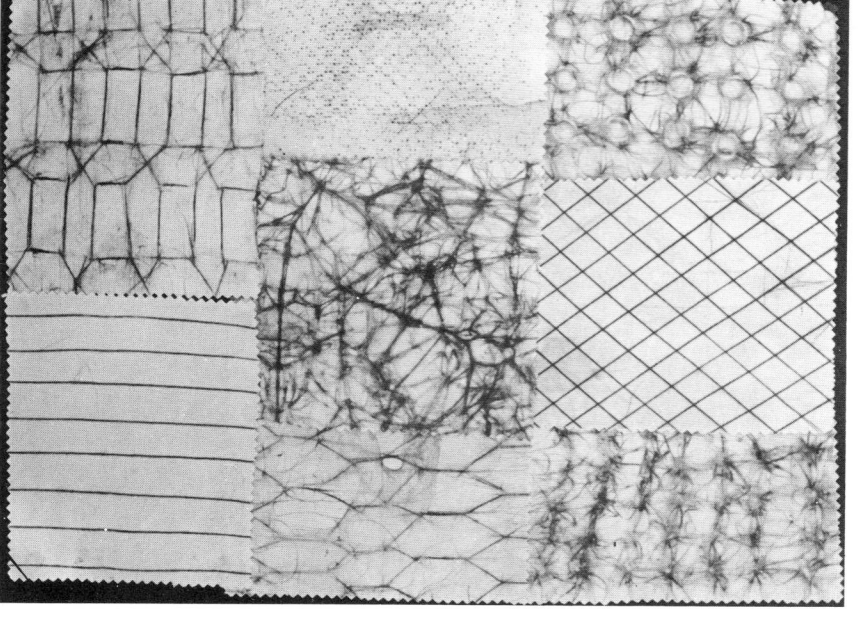

25 The cracking in these waxed samples was produced by marking lines with a sharp instrument and folding crumpling in a ball; folding over the end of a match box; rubbing over a grater; rubbing over the end of a small metal cylinder; creasing over a pencil point pushed into the fabric

The frame is assembled; then the cloth is pinned across, pulling tightly. The tighter the cloth, the better the rubbing.

For rubbing larger objects such as church gravestones or reliefs on public buildings, the frame is put together beforehand for convenience in carrying. The cloth is pinned on the sides *AB* and *CD* only, then *AC* and *BD* are removed, the fabric rolled around *AB* and *CD* and when re-assembled is pinned on the other two sides. The cloth is arranged around the winged nut in the corners. Put heavy weights at the corners to keep the cloth in position whilst making the rubbing.

Before carrying out any such form of rubbing permission should be obtained from an official in charge.

If a length of material is to be waxed, it helps to wind it on a cardboard roll which can then be unwound as required. As the work progresses, the part already waxed is put on a second roll. This is convenient in the classroom, or in a small space where a number of people work. It is also a useful way of storing waxed cloth between stages of completion, without crackling the surface too much.

Both sides of the fabric should be waxed for the best results in the dyeing process. It is important that the wax is really hot, otherwise it will sit on the cloth and the dye will slip underneath. Wax is ready for application when it makes a transparent mark on the cloth. When the waxing is complete, the fabric is ready for the dye-bath.

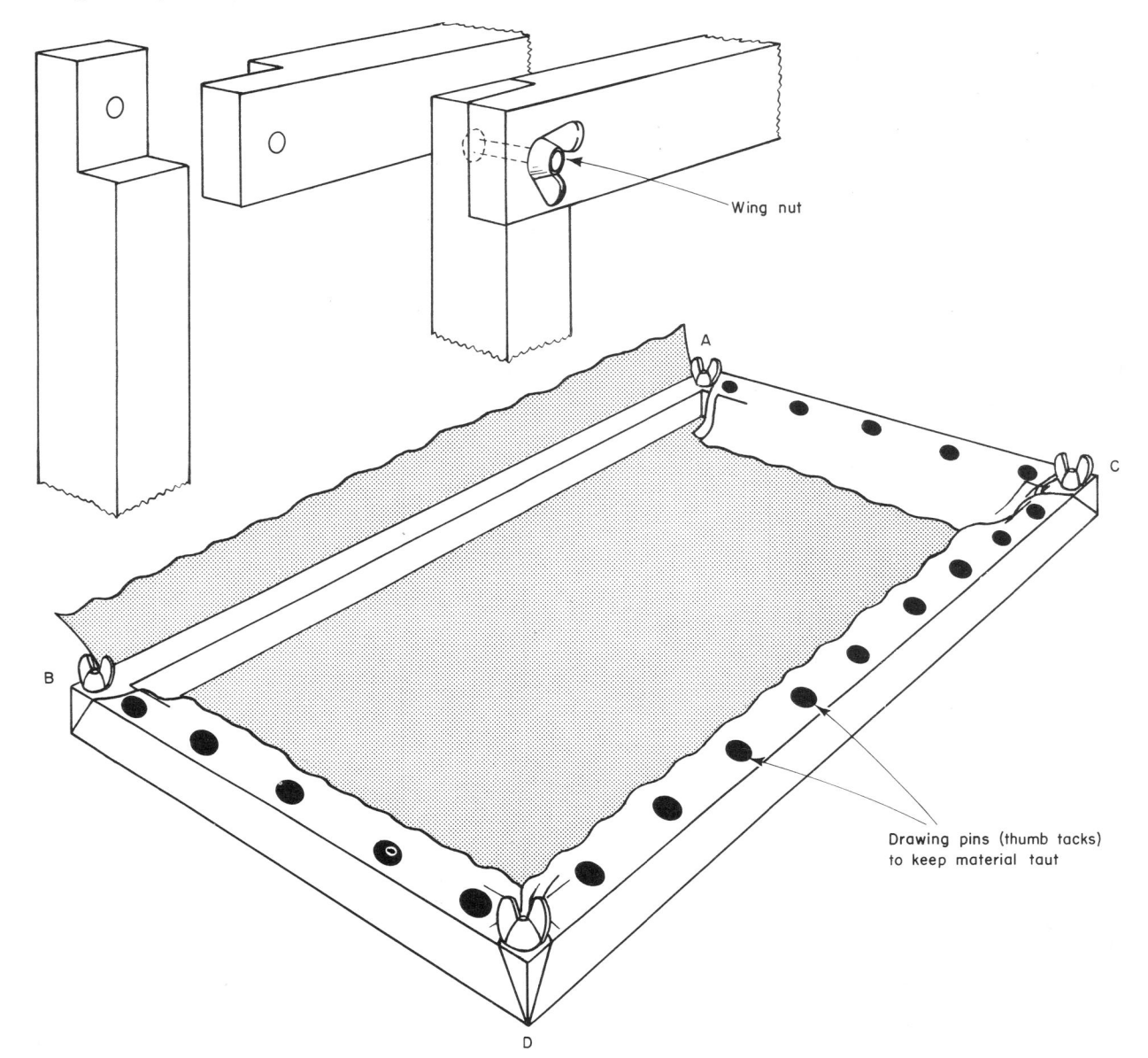

Wing nut

Drawing pins (thumb tacks) to keep material taut

26 A rubbing of the De Freville brass, Little Shelford Church, Cambridgeshire. Fine cotton lawn stretched and pinned tightly to a wooden frame made from lengths of wood bought cheaply in a hardware store, size about $\frac{5}{8}$ in. $\times$ $1\frac{1}{4}$ in. was used in making this brass rubbing. The frame was put over the brass, weights put at each corner to prevent any movement, and the figures rubbed carefully and firmly with a candle, making sure the wax was rubbed evenly over the surface of the cloth. Then the cloth was taken from the frame, and Procion grey dye, in printing paste form, was rolled over the surface. After air fixing, the cloth was boiled, dried and pressed

27 Dyeing fabric in a bowl

Dyeing a piece of fabric

Detailed instructions for dyeing a piece of fabric vary according to the dye used and the result required. However, all dyeing for batik must take place in a cool dye bath, as any heat for fixing the dye would destroy the wax design and render the pattern useless. If the wax is cracked, the dye runs in and a fine marbling texture is made.

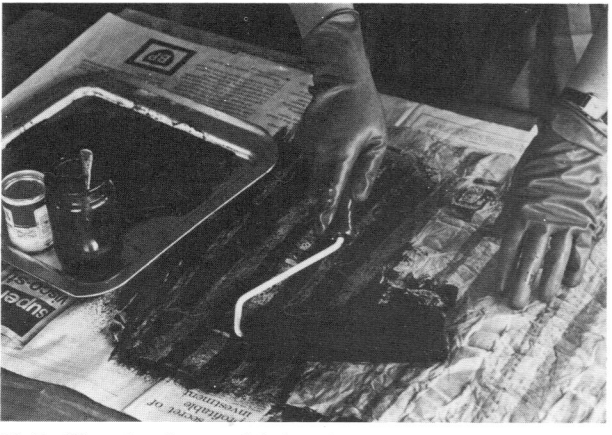

28 Rolling the dye on fabric using a
foam-rubber roller

29 Drying the dyed fabric on the flat
table top or floor on top of newspaper

If no cracking is desired the cloth must be immersed in the bath
without crumpling, or the dye brushed or rolled on with a sponge
roller.

After dyeing, the material dries more evenly if it is first laid flat on the
floor or a table top. A large sheet of polythene (polyethylene) under
sheets of newspaper on which the cloth is laid, prevents the dye from
staining the surface. When the fabric has drained on the flat surface, it
can then be blotted between newspaper and hung to dry.

The fabric is left until it is thoroughly dry, then further areas are
waxed, and the whole cloth dyed again. After two applications of wax
and dye, boil off the wax and start again. This process is repeated until
the result is satisfactory, then the wax is removed.

The removal of wax

Heat the water in a large saucepan or bath. When the water boils the
waxed cloth is put in and moved about gently for not more than three
minutes, then it is lifted out and dropped into a bucket of cold water.
The wax solidifies immediately. After squeezing out the water, the wax
is shaken off. With the addition of ½ teaspoonful of Lissapol (U.K.),
Synthrapol SP (U.S.A.) or detergent in the boiling water, this process
is repeated twice or until there is no trace of wax left in the cloth. The
fabric is then washed in soapy water, rinsed and dried.

30 Squeezing flour and water paste from a plastic slip tracer on to the cloth

Wax can also be removed by ironing the fabric with a hot iron between sheets of blotting paper, or newspaper, which must be changed frequently. However, by this method the fabric never seems to be really free of wax, and remains rather stiff, particularly when resin is used.

After the liquid has cooled, the wax boiled off the fabric for the first time before Lissapol is added can be reclaimed as it rises from the surface and forms a crust which is easily removed. This wax can be added in small quantities to the new wax and melted down.

NEVER pour water containing wax down a sink as it will cause a blockage.

Paste resist

Some Javanese and African textiles are dyed using a paste resist called cassava paste. A very effective paste similar to this resist is made by mixing flour and water.

Equipment

Fork
Flour
Basin
Plastic slip tracer as used in pottery or a plastic detergent bottle which can squirt or dribble liquid through a small opening in its cap.

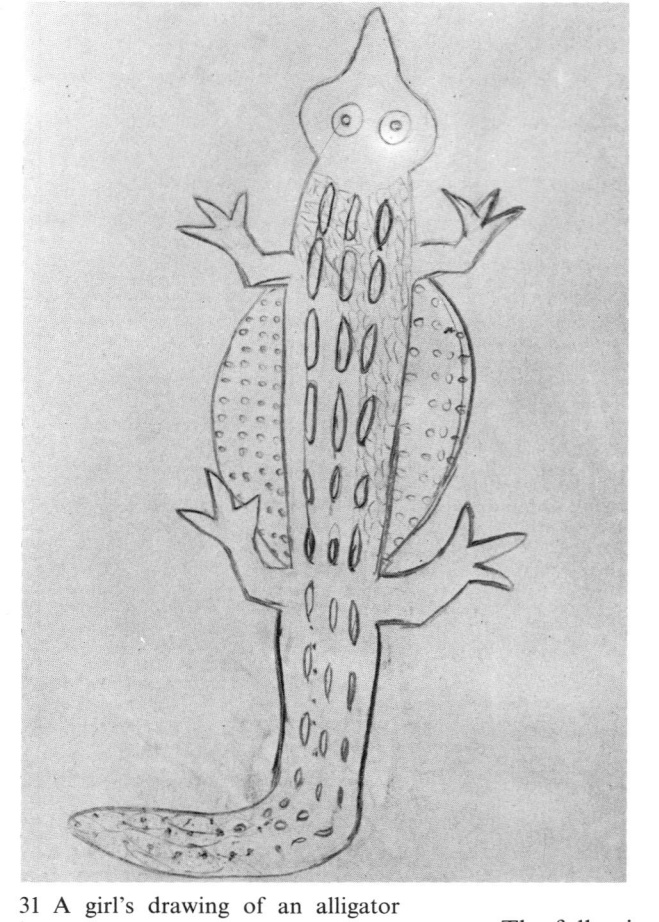

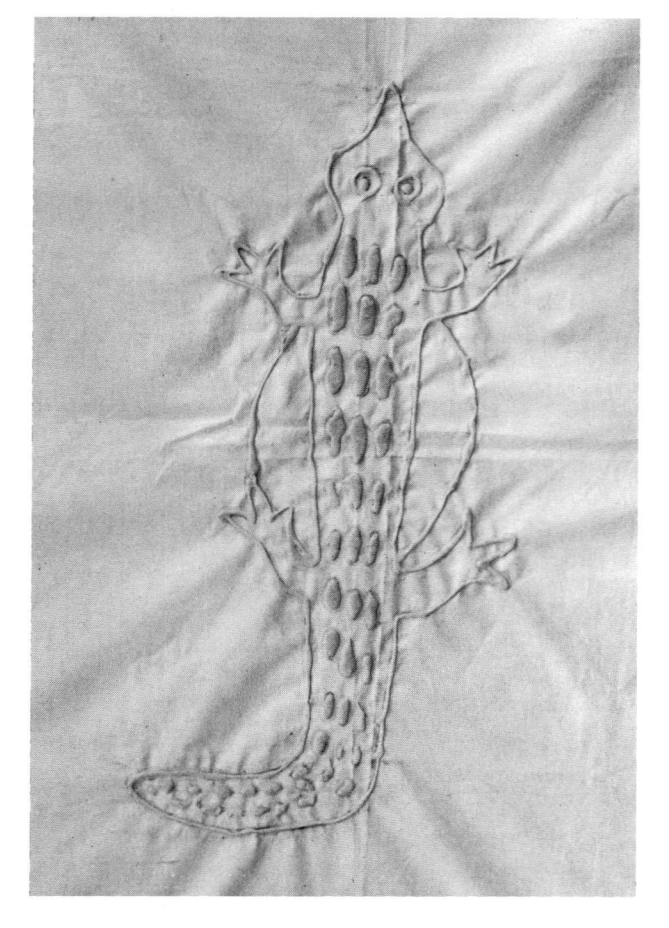

31 A girl's drawing of an alligator inspired by an Aboriginal painting

32 The animal is traced on to the cloth in pencil and outlined with a trail of flour and water paste, then dried

The following instructions are for decorating a piece of cloth, using a paste resist and Printex (Tinolite) Fabric Printing Colour.

Designs are transferred to the cloth by using a cardboard stencil drawn round lightly with chalk or charcoal or by tracing.

Using ordinary household flour (plain or self raising) add water to it until a moderately thin paste is produced which drops easily from the prongs of a fork. Approximately 1 tablespoonful of flour to $\frac{1}{3}$ pint of water. Then mix well to disperse all lumps.

Fill a slip tracer or plastic detergent container with the paste and cover all the areas which are not to be dyed and allow to dry thoroughly (overnight if possible).

33 The dye is worked into the surface
with brushes and sponges

Using 2 in. to 3 in. decorators' brushes, with small circular move-
ments, apply the palest colour of the dye evenly all over the cloth,
leaving no residue on the surface. Try to force the dye into the fibres of
the cotton. Allow to dry thoroughly. Next cover the area to be reserved
in that colour with a further application of paste—allow to dry, then,
using the brushes and the next colour, apply as before and allow to
dry. These processes are repeated until the pattern and colour scheme
is complete.

When the last coat of the dye is completed allow it to dry thoroughly.

Remove the paste from the cloth with a round-ended knife—
avoiding unpasted areas to prevent damaging the dye before it is heat
fixed.

34 Detail from the finished fabric after applications of yellow, orange and blue dye. See colour plate

Iron on the wrong side several times with the heat control dial at 'linen' heat and then turn the cloth on to the right side and iron with the control dial at 'cotton' heat. The longer the cloth is ironed the more permanent the dye will become.

Wash the fabric without rubbing. Just immerse the cloth several times in detergent with water, then rinse well.

Allow to drip dry, and then iron.

The recipe for Printex dye is on page 39.

These paste-resist patterns are particularly satisfactory with younger pupils as there is no danger from hot wax or lighted candles.

35 Flour and water paste is spread over the cloth then designs scratched through it with sharp tools, and left to dry

36 Result after dyeing and removing paste resist

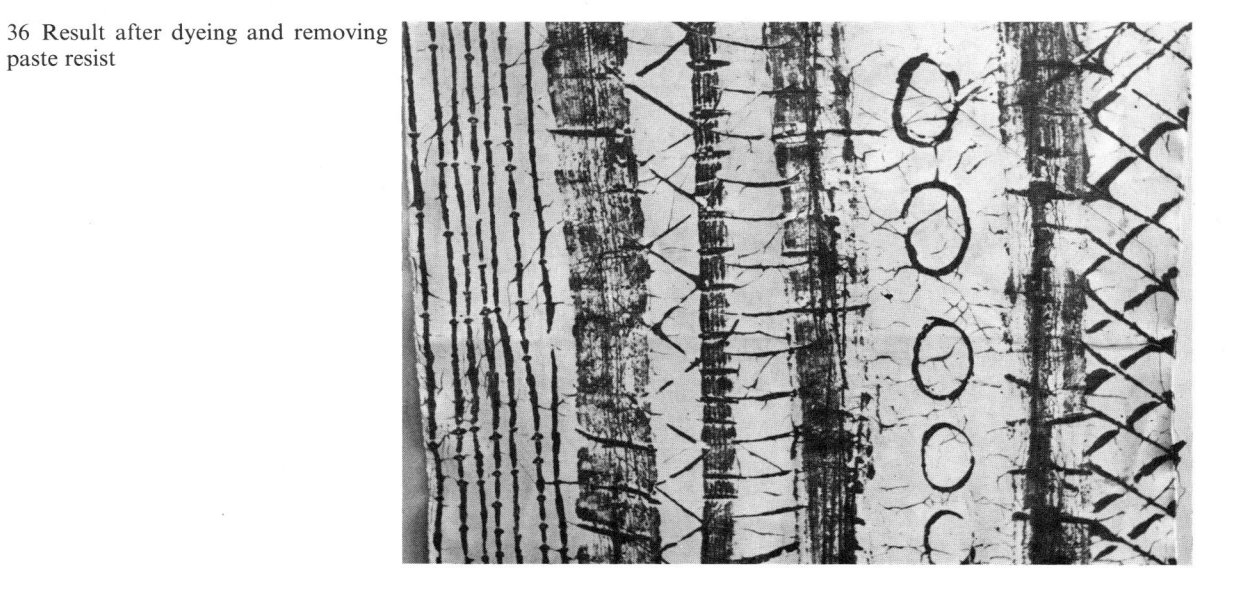

The dyes

All dyes used must be effective in cold water, as any heat needed for fixing a colour would melt the wax and render the pattern useless. Some primitive dyes are useful for experiments and classroom work. They produce pleasing results without too many complicated processes. The colours, however, are not fast to sunlight and constant washing.

Potassium permanganate crystals

These crystals can be bought cheaply at any chemist's shop and give a khaki-brown dye.

Recipe

1 teaspoonful of permanganate crystals dissolved in 1 pint warm water. Stir and leave to cool.

Dip the waxed cloth in the solution, or paint on with a brush.

The pink-brown turns to brown as the cloth dries. Repeat the waxing, dipping and drying; each dip makes the cloth one tone deeper. Remove the wax by boiling. Rinse and wash. Wash the brush thoroughly after using this dye as if allowed to stand in the liquid, the bristles are destroyed.

Indigo vat

There are many recipes for this dye vat. Here is one that I have found satisfactory.

In a large container measure $4\frac{1}{2}$ gallons of warm water. Sprinkle 1 oz sodium hydrosulphite on the surface and stir gently. This removes the air from the water.

In a glass or enamel bowl put in the following order

8 oz salt

3 oz caustic soda previously dissolved in $\frac{1}{2}$ lb jar of water

4 oz sodium hydrosulphite

$\frac{1}{2}$ lb indigo grains

2 pints warm water

Stir as each ingredient is added. This makes the stock solution.

CAUTION

Always add the caustic soda to the liquid. NEVER the reverse.

Lower this stock solution into the vat and empty the bowl without making any splashes which would introduce oxygen and weaken the strength of the dye.

After 15 minutes the vat is ready for use.

By dipping out a little of the solution into a small jar, check that the solution under the blue-bronze crust which forms is a clear yellow-green liquid.

Wet the material to be dyed in water to which a teaspoonful of Lissapol has been added. Shake out to remove excess water. This prevents cracking the wax too much. Gently lower the material into the vat, taking care not to create air bubbles. Keep the cloth submerged for two minutes. (A large stone can be tied in a bag, then pinned to the bottom of the cloth and used as a weight.) Remove from the vat, again making no drips. Spread the cloth out to oxidize for three minutes. It will change in colour from yellow-green to dark blue. Return the cloth to the vat for one more minute. After removing, spread out to dry on a newspaper-covered polythene sheet. When dry rinse the cloth in cold water to remove excess dye and then boil out the wax.

Cold water dyes: Dylon (U.K.), Tintex or Aljo Batik dye (U.S.A.)

Use according to the instructions on the tin.

For instance, for ½ lb weight material

   dissolve one small tin of dye in 1 pint warm water

In a separate container put

   4 tablespoonfuls salt

   1 tablespoonful soda, dissolved in 1 pint hot water.

When cool mix these solutions in equal quantities, and paint on, or immerse the waxed fabric in the dye. Leave for ½ hour or more, then remove. Dry the cloth.

If a further dye is needed, wax the areas and repeat the process of dyeing.

When dyeing is complete, rinse thoroughly until the water clears, cover with boiling water, plus detergent, or put in a saucepan of boiling water and detergent, then wash and dry.

Procion dyes

The 'M' Range of Procion dyes is most suitable for batik work as they are air fixed and so need no extra heat process for fixing before the wax is boiled off. The colours are clear, bright and fast once they are finally fixed. They mix together to produce various tones and new colours by the addition of even the smallest quantities of dye one to another. The following colours are suggested as a basic range

Yellow	M 4RS (gold-yellow)
Yellow	M 6GS (lemon-yellow)
Brilliant red	M 8BS (blue-red)
Blue	M 3RS (navy)
Blue	M 3GS (green-blue)
Brilliant orange M 2RS.	

Also useful are

Grey	M GS (grey-blue)
Red-brown	M 4RS (rich chestnut).

Before beginning any serious work, it is advisable to experiment with colours on small pieces of the fabric, record quantities and qualities of the dyes, and so build up a colour reference record.

Procion dyes take well on pure cotton and linen and silk fabrics. On cottons with special finishes, and containing man-made fibres, the colours are pale, so it is best to avoid these when choosing fabrics for dyeing in school.

Recipe for Procion dye bath

There are many recipes for a Procion dye bath. Here is a recipe that has been found most successful on cotton lawn, calico, linen, silk and wool and cotton mixtures.

Dissolve $\frac{1}{2}$ to 5 level teaspoonfuls of dye in $\frac{1}{2}$ pint warm water.

Add just over 5 tablespoonfuls of common, or cooking salt, dissolved in 2 pints cold water.

Place the cloth in the bath and leave for 6 minutes, turning from time to time.

Then add a bare 2 level tablespoonfuls of washing soda (also known as Salsoda in the U.S.A.) dissolved in 2 tablespoonfuls of warm water.

Leave the cloth in the dye bath for a further 15 minutes, turning occasionally.

Remove from the bath and drain.

Lay fabric on newspaper and polythene to dry. Re-wax.

Repeat this routine after each waxing, remembering that wax deteriorates after two dips.

After the final dye, leave to dry for 24 hours.

Finally rinse off loose dye in cold water, until it runs clear, then boil in a saucepan to which $\frac{1}{2}$ teaspoonful of Lissapol has been added for 2 to 3 minutes, and wash in warm soapy water before drying and ironing.

When the soda is added the dye reacts quickly and it is essential that the dye is on the fabric in the dye bath before the soda is added.

This quantity dyes 2 to 3 yards of fabric, according to the weight of cloth. The recipe can be multiplied or divided for larger or smaller lengths of material.

The recipe works well, even if the measurement of salt, dye and soda are not exact, though for repeating an exact colour, the measurements would have to be accurate.

Once the soda has been added to the solution the dye reacts and cannot be kept.

Some batik designs are made by waxing the outline of a design with a tjanting or thin brush, and painting in one of the areas with dye. The painted areas are then waxed when dry to retain the colour and the whole fabric dipped in a dye bath to colour the background.

37 Waxing over the design, after the pattern has been painted with a thin form of printing paste. The heat from the hot wax helps to fix the dye

38 Detail from the scarf after it has been dipped in brilliant red dye, waxed, cracked and put in Brentamine Fast Black K Salt. See colour plate

When painting with dye it is more satisfactory to use a thin solution of Procion dye printing paste. This makes the dye easier to handle as the ordinary dye solution tends to creep along the threads and spread through any cracks made in the wax.

Recipe for Procion dye printing paste
To prepare Manutex RS (U.K.), Keltex (U.S.A.) binder or sodium alginate thickener put 1 teaspoonful of calgon in
   1 pint of water.
   Sprinkle in 1 level tablespoonful of Manutex, stirring all the time.
   Leave to stand until it is smooth and transparent.
   Next, in a jar put 10 parts (10 level teaspoonfuls) urea, dissolved in $46/42\frac{1}{2}$ (12 tablespoonfuls) parts water.
   Add 1 to 5 parts Procion dyestuffs according to shade required.
   This is then stirred into 20 parts (5 tablespoonfuls) of Manutex RS 5% thickening (a printing paste needs 40 parts Manutex).
   Add 1 part (1 teaspoonful) Resist Salt L.

When cool, and just before painting, add $1\frac{1}{2}$ parts ($1\frac{1}{2}$ teaspoonfuls) bicarbonate of soda.

Once the bicarbonate of soda is added the dye reacts and the mixture will remain potent for only an hour or two. Therefore it is best to make a jar of dye paste and use only small quantities (about $\frac{1}{16}$th) at a time, adding the bicarbonate in $\frac{1}{4}$ teaspoonfuls as required if only small areas are to be painted.

For very small quantities of a number of dyes, a jar of the urea, Manutex, resist salt and water is made using the previous recipe. This is added as required to $\frac{1}{4}$ teaspoonful of dye powder in small containers and stirred well. Add the bicarbonate of soda before painting.

After fixing by air hanging, the wax is boiled off and the material then washed and dried.

Interesting colours and variations are made if after the final dye the cloth is re-waxed and dipped into a solution of Brentamine Fast Black K Salt. This produces a rich brown colour, typical of many Javanese batiks.

Brentamine Fast Black K Salt (U.K.) Fast Black K Salt (U.S.A.)

Dissolve about $\frac{1}{2}$ teaspoonful of K Salt in a cup of warm water. Allow to cool, then immerse the dry fabric, after the final dye, but before washing off. When the cloth is dry, remove and wax, and fix dye in the usual manner of boiling in water.

Printex Fabric Printing Colour

This is the name under which small quantities of Tinolite dyes can be bought for schools. It is a pigment dye and in this book it has been used with paste-resist designs.

Recipe for Printex dye (Tinolite)
1 cup of binder.
1 teaspoonful of pigment (for pastel shades use less pigment).
When using in paste-resist patterns, $\frac{1}{8}$th of a cupful of water is added to the mixture for the first application of dye, $\frac{1}{16}$th of a cupful of water for the second application, and no water at all for the third.
2 cupfuls of dye mixture are adequate for a 3 yard length of 36 in. material.

Procion dyes, in 'painting' paste form (less Manutex binder) are also successful with flour and water paste resist.

The dye must be worked into the cloth with a brush or small piece of sponge.

After removing the paste from the cloth, the dye is fixed by ironing with a hot iron for 3 to 5 minutes before boiling, washing and ironing. Procion dyes leave the cloth soft and pliable, as the dye reacts and becomes part of the cloth fibre.

Indigosol dyes

These dyes can be obtained in a range of clear bright colours and are successful on cotton, linen or silk. Follow the instructions carefully because there may be some variation according to the product. These colours are very fast and must be kept in the dark when not in use. There is also some variation according to the fabric being used.

Recipe for ½ yard material
1 teaspoon of dye dissolved in
½ a cupful of warm water.
Paint this liquid on to the fabric with a brush. Hang out to dry but avoid strong light. At this stage the colours are deceptive. The dry cloth is then immersed in a fixing solution when the true colours appear.

Fixing solution
To 1 pint of warm water add
½ a teaspoonful of sodium nitrite and
4 tablespoonfuls of diluted sulphuric acid.

Wash out the cloth throughly in warm soapy water, rinse, dry and press.

CAUTION Sulphuric acid is extremely dangerous. When diluting it, always add the acid to the water in a thin stream. Wear rubber gloves to protect the hands while fixing the dyes.

To dilute sulphuric acid add 3 fluid ounces of sulphuric acid to 1 quart of cold water.

See 38

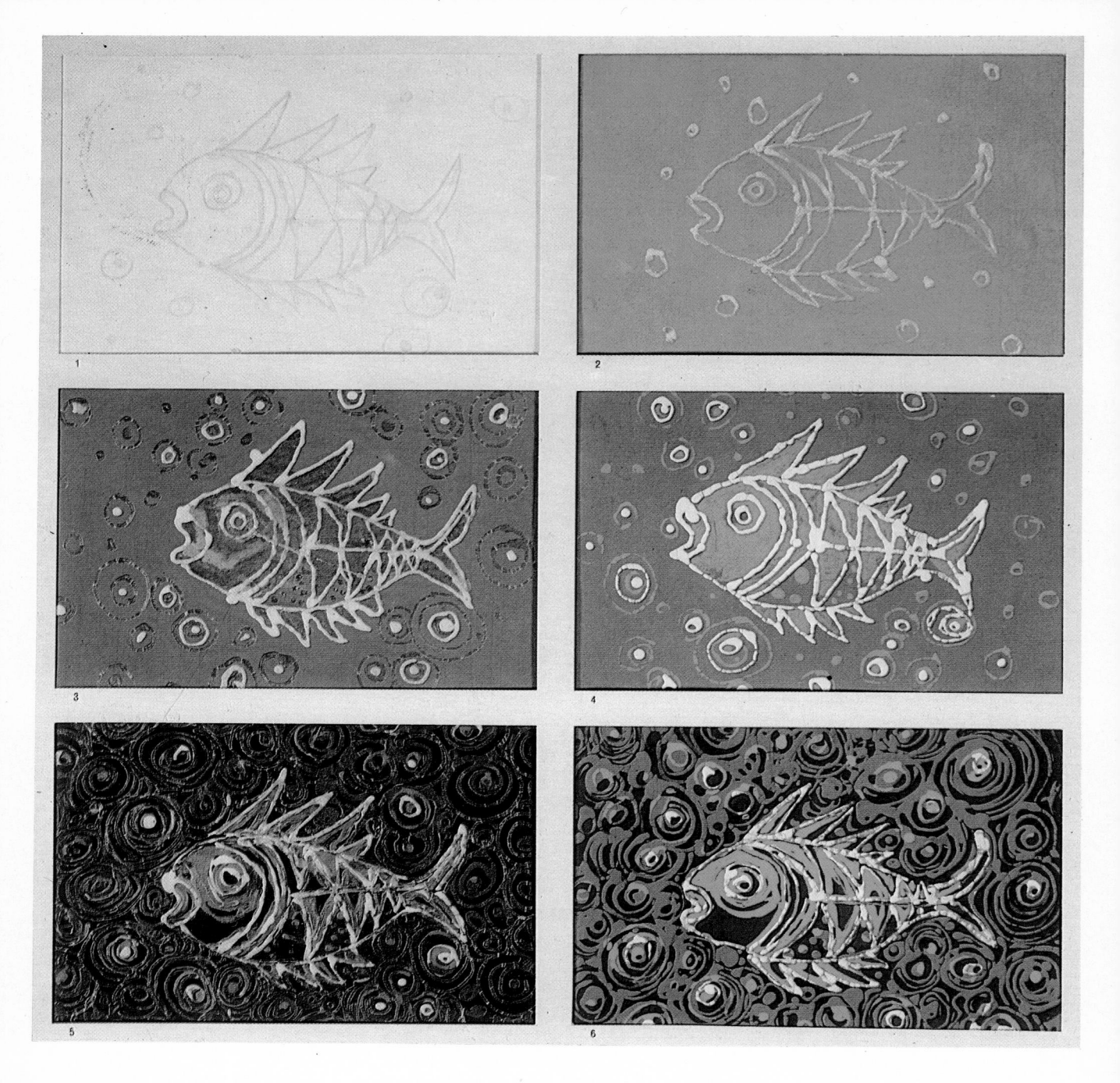

◄ *Waxing and dyeing a piece of fabric with Procion dyes*
1 Design drawn on the fabric and waxed
2 First dye bath—blue
3 Waxing of new areas and dyed yellow
4 Wax boiled off
5 Re-waxing of design, and new areas, and dyed in dark blue
6 Wax boiled off, and fabric washed and ironed

Some reasons for disappointing results in waxing and dyeing

a The wax may not be hot enough, so the dye penetrates the fabric under the wax.

b The wax may be too hot for certain fabrics. It is important to get the wax to the right temperature or it will become too fluid and spread on contact with the cloth, and the design will become uneven. A scrap of material is useful for trying out the flow of wax and preventing too many variations when these are not intended.

c The wax is damaged if it has been pulled away from the working surface. The dye penetrates these areas—particularly the Procion dyes.

d The definition of the wax pattern is spoiled if the dye bath is warm, or if the wax on the cloth is not hard. To harden wax, put in cold air, run under a cold water tap, or put in a refrigerator before dyeing. This improves the crackle.

e After two dips in *Procion* dye, the wax disintegrates and the dye penetrates the fabric and the fine pattern is destroyed. It is best, therefore, to boil off the wax and re-wax the design before continuing the dyeing process.

f If too much of the design is waxed at the beginning, large areas of white will be produced, leaving little opportunity for development with further colours if this is intended. However, if large areas are waxed, and the cloth dyed with the darkest colour (after boiling off, and re-waxing), dyeing can be carried out in a reverse process, from dark to light, with interesting results, boiling off each time, and reducing the wax areas.

g If the cloth is left to boil too long the fabric may re-absorb the loose dye and the colours become muddy.

h If the dye is not sufficiently fixed before the wax is boiled off the colours may be pale.

i The quality of the reclaimed wax may have been destroyed by containing too much detergent.

If the final result of waxing and dyeing does not please, most of the Dylon and Procion colours can be removed by boiling the fabric in a solution of colour remover. After a thorough wash and rinse, waxing and dyeing can start all over again. This does not apply to pigment dye.

39 Sea urchins, coral, stripes on stone and shells

Sources of inspiration for pattern and design

Natural objects are an endless source of pattern, colour and design inspiration. Stones and shells, tree bark, seeds, leaves and plants all offer a starting point, and the designs develop as the stages of dyeing progress.

Visits to all types of museums provide excellent opportunities for studying patterns used by primitive peoples on their pottery, weapons, jewellery and carvings.

Photographs of buildings, demolition, stacks of tins, or industrial material, wooden blocks, chairs in school, pavements, bricks, wheels; all can be utilised as a basis of a design in colour, shape and pattern. The possibilities are endless.

40 Fir cones, feathers and bark

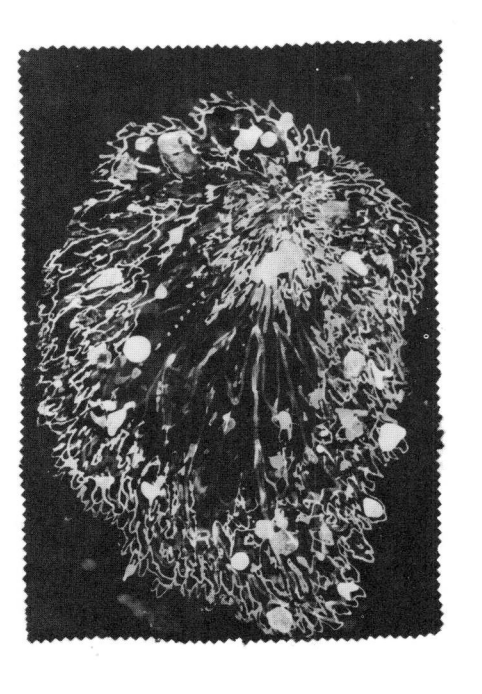

41 The design using the shape of a Begonia Rex leaf was drawn freely with a tjanting, dyed yellow, re-waxed, and dyed grey. The fabric was then boiled, washed and ironed (Procion). See colour plate

42 Detail of a scarf. The white silk had trails of wax marked on, dyed pink, printed using the texture of a car sponge, in orange-brown, and finally a leaf shape cut out of brown paper and stencilled on with a brush and purple dye (Procion)

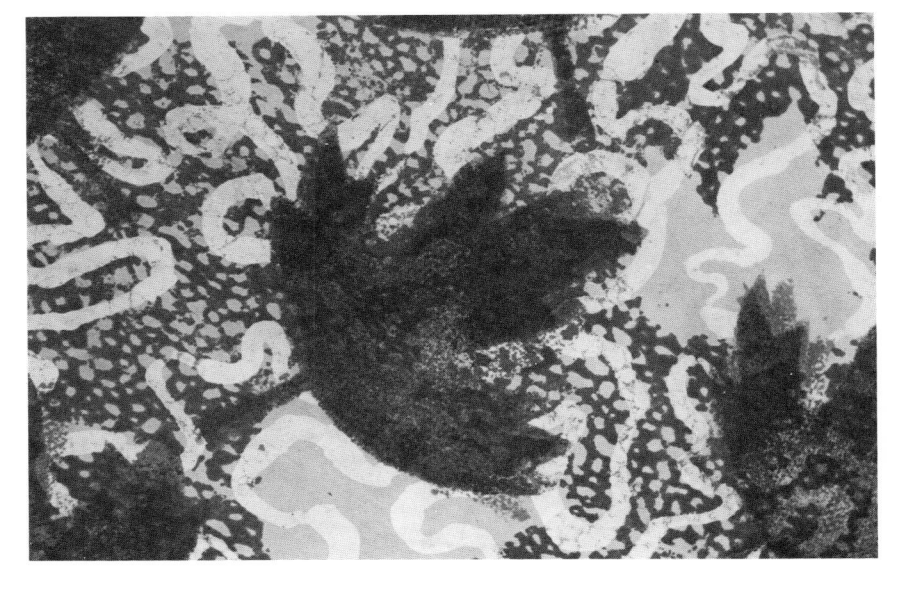

43 Design for a hanging using snow-flake pattern. This was made using a flour and water paste resist, and Printex dyes, in shades of white, pink, pale blue and dark blue

44 A fish and skeleton using flour and water paste-resist method in white, yellow-orange, green and purple Print-ex dyes

45 Detail of a fire-bird, in flour and water paste resist in white, pinks and reds, and Printex dyes. See colour plate

See 50

46 Sketches made by girls during a visit to the Museum of Anthropology in Cambridge, England. They were made mostly in the South Sea Islands Section

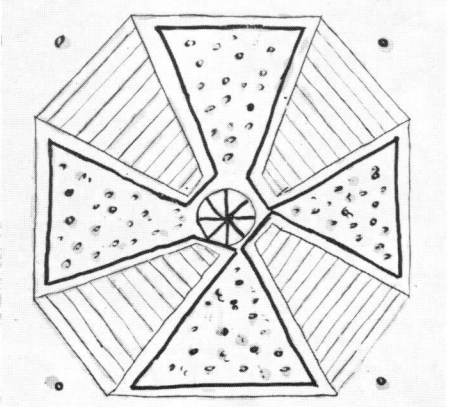

47–9 Each girl chose a design from the sketch and enlarged it, inked in the outline, and used it as a guide under the fabric while waxing. The squares were waxed, first dyed yellow, waxed, dyed orange, waxed then dyed purple (Procion)

50 After the squares were all sewn together, a border was printed with potato blocks in black Procion printing paste (5 parts blue 3GS to 1 part brilliant orange 2RS) on a plain red-brown border, and round the squares. See colour plate

51 A native-shield shape was used to decorate this fabric. This was made with flour and water paste resist, and Printex dyes, of yellow, orange and brown

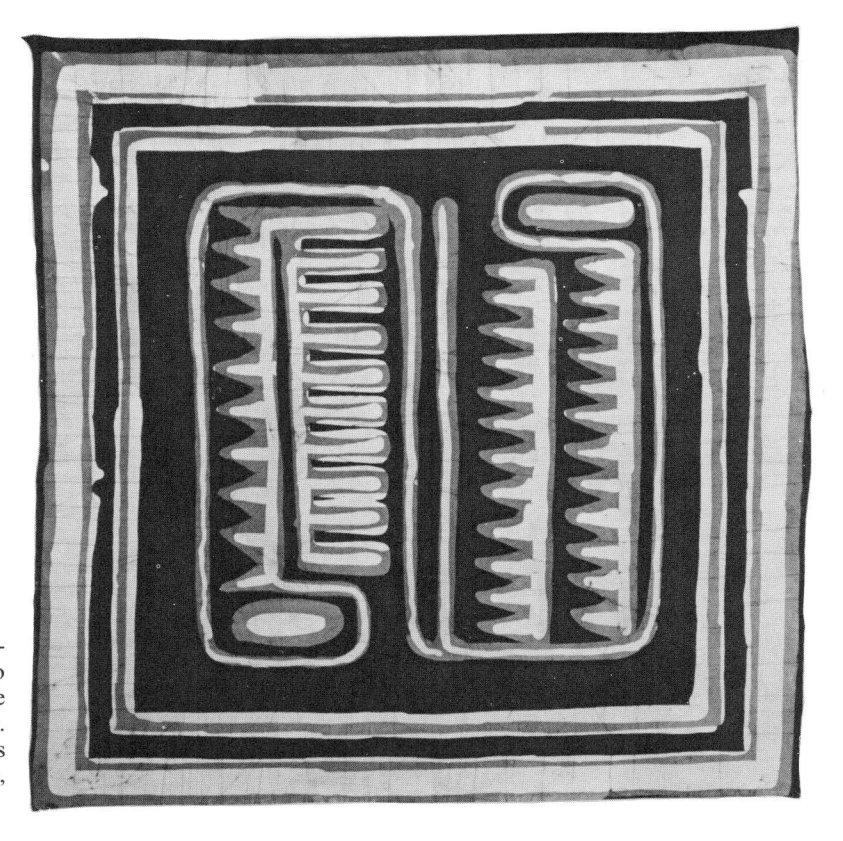

52 A square incorporating a Mexican-inspired design and dyed from dark to light in colour. Large areas were waxed, and the fabric dyed dark blue. The wax was boiled off. The fabric was then re-waxed, exposing areas of white, and dyed a tan colour (Procion)

53 This is a cotton bedspread made by a group of 14-year-old girls after studying the patterns of the African Indigo hanging. They each designed two squares, one an overall pattern, the other a single unit design. The squares all had a 1 in. border. First the squares were dyed orange, re-waxed, dyed brilliant red, re-waxed and finally dyed navy-blue. After the wax was removed, the squares were sewn together to form a satisfactory design (Procion)

54 A stack of logs photographed in a railway siding in Switzerland

55 A silk scarf using the pattern made by the logs. The circles were drawn in with a tjanting, and painted with thin Procion printing paste, in shades of yellow and red-brown. The logs were then waxed all over, and cracks scratched in the surface of the wax with a knitting needle. The scarf was dipped in Procion red-brown dye, dried and then Brentamine Fast Black K Salt, and when dry, the wax was boiled off

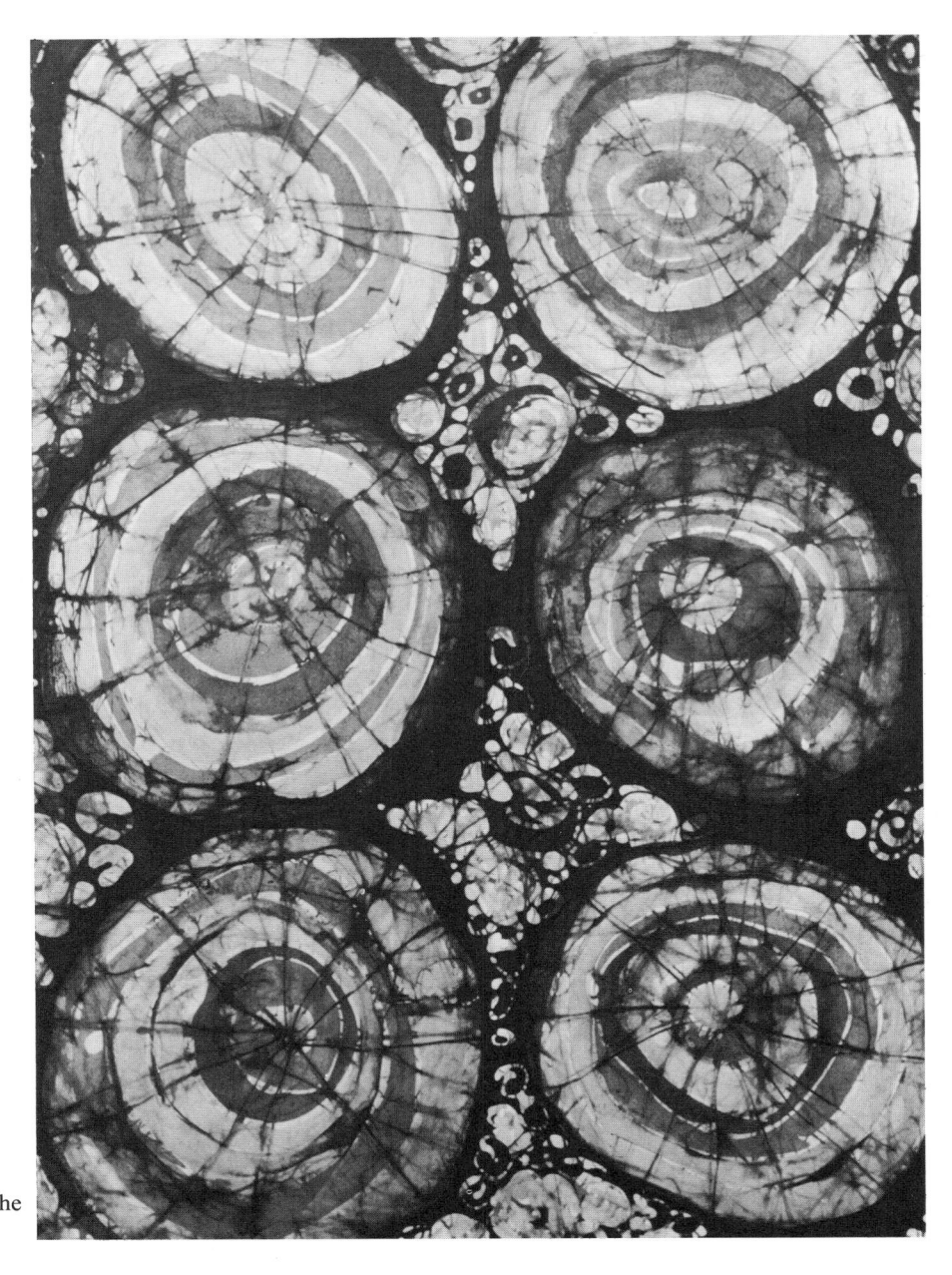

56 A detail of the scarf showing the cracks

57 This is an indigo paste-resist fabric from Nigeria. It was the inspiration for the wax-resist hanging using Procion dyes, produced by a group of girls

◄ Variety in treatment of a Begonia Rex leaf

The leaf was drawn with the tjanting, and the dye painted on in different areas.

Then the whole leaf was waxed, and dipped in a yellow-grey dye.

This was waxed all over when dry—crumpled, and put in Brentamine Fast Black K Salt, then boiled, washed and ironed.

The leaf was painted freely with Procion dye in thin printing paste form.

When dry the leaf was waxed and the background dyed.

The background was waxed and crumpled, and put in Brentamine Fast Black K Salt.

After boiling, washing and dyeing the leaf was used as a basis for machine embroidery with an ordinary sewing machine. See also 41.

58 Another hanging made by a group of girls, this time dyed light blue, dark blue, and finally brilliant red. A decorative border was added in material dyed light blue (Procion)

59 A picture in turquoise-blue, light blue, and dark blue, suggested by the shapes of eastern minarets and palaces (Procion)

60 A child's dress in yellow and pink with plain facings. The fabric was first waxed all over, cracked and dyed yellow. The wax was boiled off and the cloth re-waxed all over, cracked and dyed Procion brilliant red. The plain facings were made from unwaxed material dyed with the yellow then the brilliant-red dye. They then matched perfectly

Uses for the fabrics

Always experiment with fabrics to test the dyes and designs before embarking on a serious piece of work. When the patterning is planned, the purpose of the fabric should be clear from the start.

The design becomes an integral part of the work. For a scarf, cushion, curtain or bedspread the design has to be planned to suit the size and purpose of the finished article. Dresses and blouses are cut from lengths of material after the waxing and dyeing has become completed though special areas of pattern such as at the neck, front or hem can be designed if the main dress pattern is marked out on the fabric.

61 A blouse in blue and grey. The wax was painted on in stripes of varying widths between each dye process (Procion)

62 A shirt blouse in white, brilliant pink and red-brown, dyed with Procion dye. The wax was painted in spots and stripes by brushes of varying widths

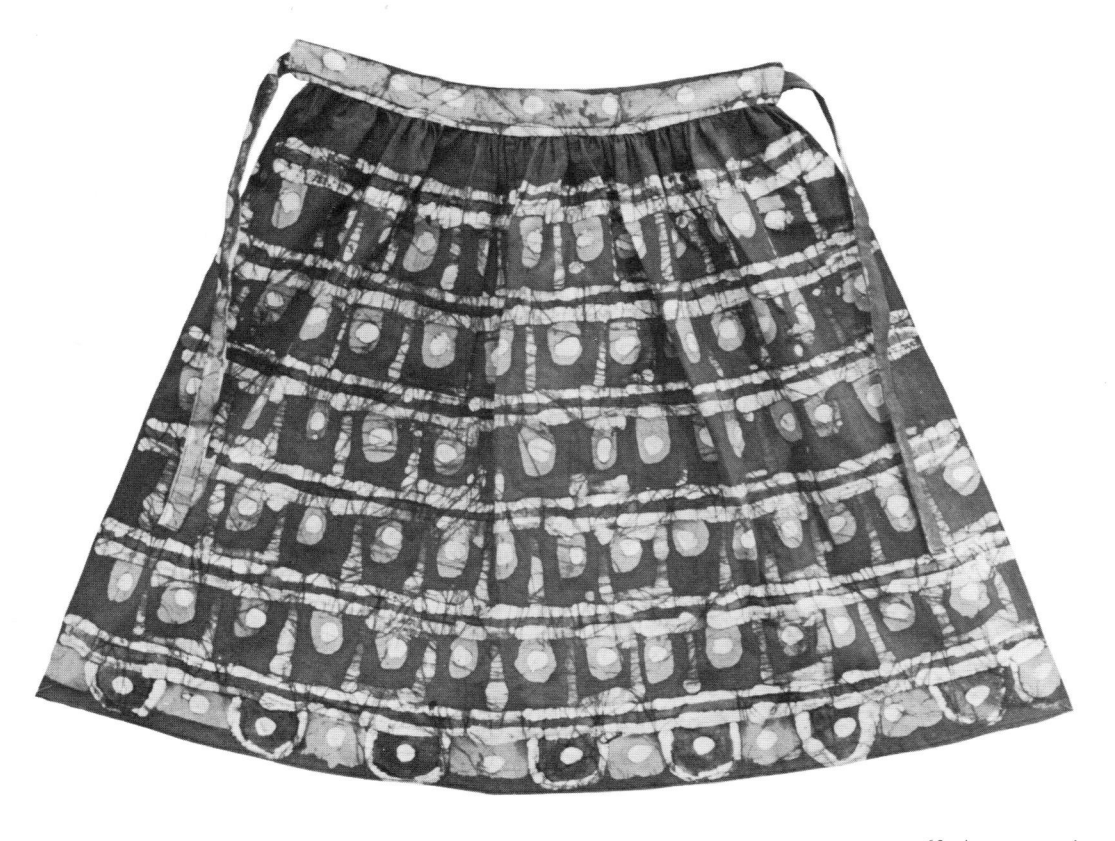

63 An apron in yellow, orange and brown made by a 14-year-old girl. The cloth was waxed; dyed yellow, re-waxed and dyed orange; re-waxed and dyed blue. The orange and blue dye made a brown (Procion)

64 A child's feeder in orange and brown. The design was waxed on cloth with a brush and tjanting, dyed orange. Further areas were waxed, and the cloth dyed in blue dye, changing the background colour to brown

65 An apron on a cotton and silk cloth in orange and red-brown illustrating a free use of the tjanting (Procion)

66 A cushion in white, blue, pink and purple made by a 13-year-old girl using a brush for the application of wax. The pattern was drawn on the fabric, and the parts to remain white were waxed. The fabric was then dyed (Procion dyes) pale blue, re-waxed and dyed a darker shade of blue. Next the wax was boiled off and the design re-waxed leaving parts of the white and blue areas uncovered, then the cloth was dyed brilliant red. The uncovered areas changed from white or blue to pink or purple. This method was used to make the wall hanging (57)

67 A silk scarf dyed in light blue, grey, and after boiling off the wax the design was painted on the fabric with a brush and the scarf dipped in an indigo vat. Finally the wax was boiled off and the silk washed, dried and ironed

68 An apron in turquoise, blue and purple using a brush and tjanting to apply the wax and employing methods of both outlining in wax and painting in Procion printing paste and waxing and dipping in the dye.

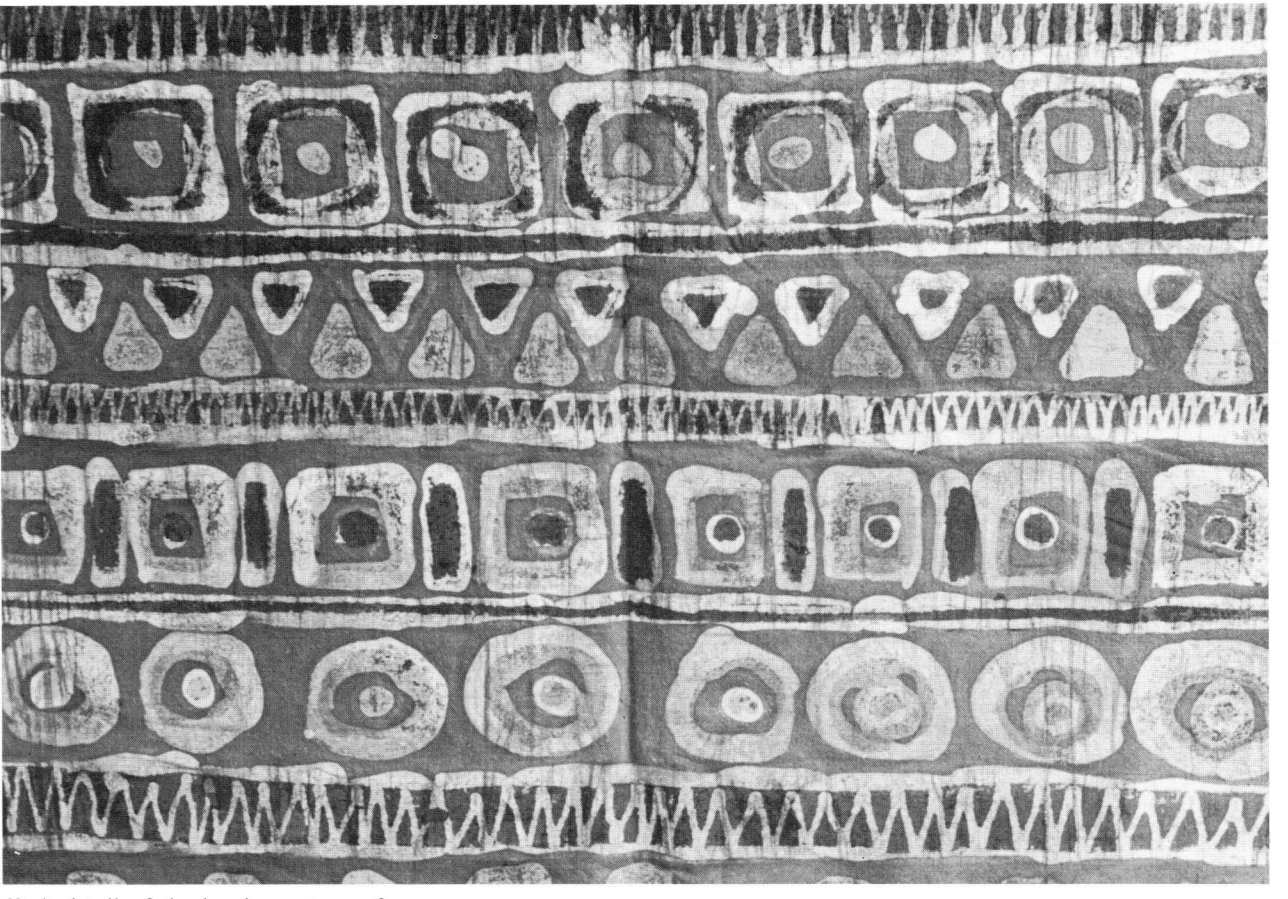

69 A detail of the border pattern of
the apron.

70 A doll's apron. This is a miniature of the overall made from the following pattern

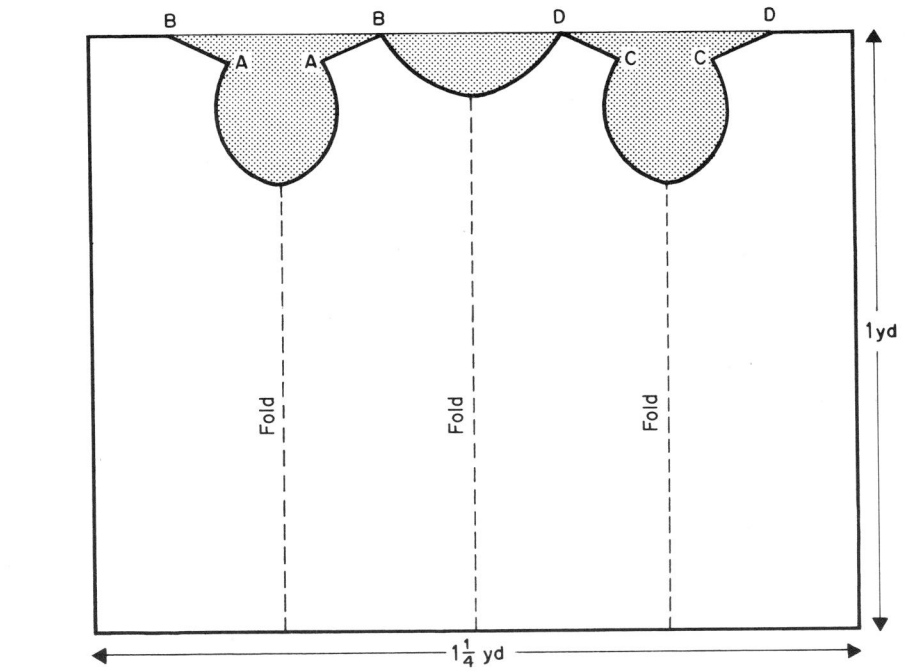

Fold into four
Mark neck and armholes
Leave back neckline straight

The overall opened out flat

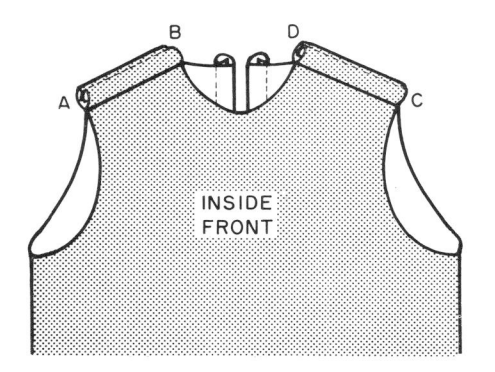

Sew shoulder seams AB and CD
Turn in edge at centre back, and hem
Turn up bottom edge, and hem

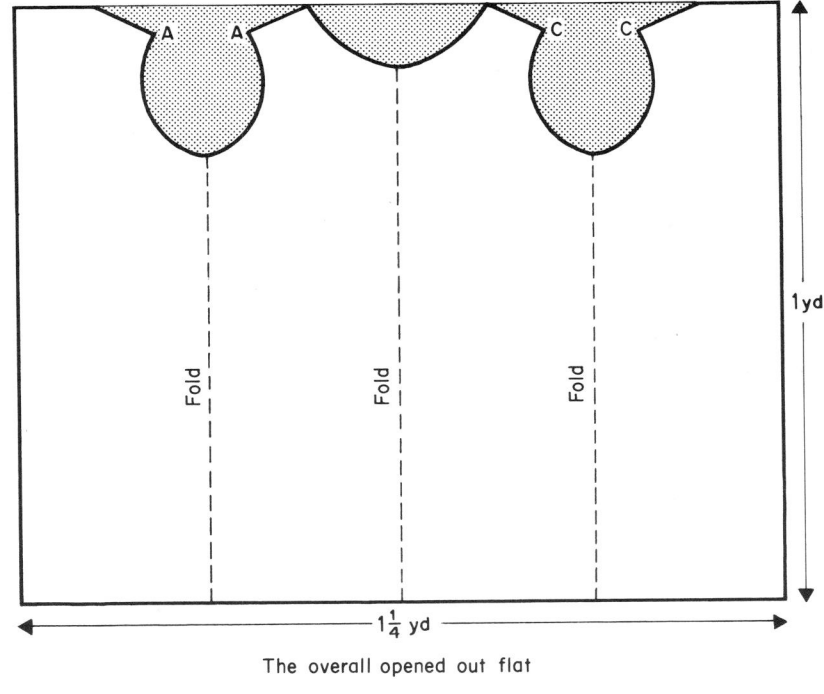

Bind neck and armholes
Make a loop at the back of the neck
Sew on button

69

71 A sun hat in yellow, orange and
green trimmed with fringing (Procion)

To make

1 Make a paper pattern from the diagram
2 Cut out two pieces in fabric and one in interlining
3 Put the right sides of the material together and the interlining on top and tack round the outside curved edge *AB* and the two straight edges *AC* leaving *CD* open
4 Trim seam and turn to right side
5 Snip small curved edge *CD* and turn in. Oversew with small stitches
6 Punch holes and fit eyelets *EF*. Fix a tape inside *GH*
7 Decorate with fringing if required

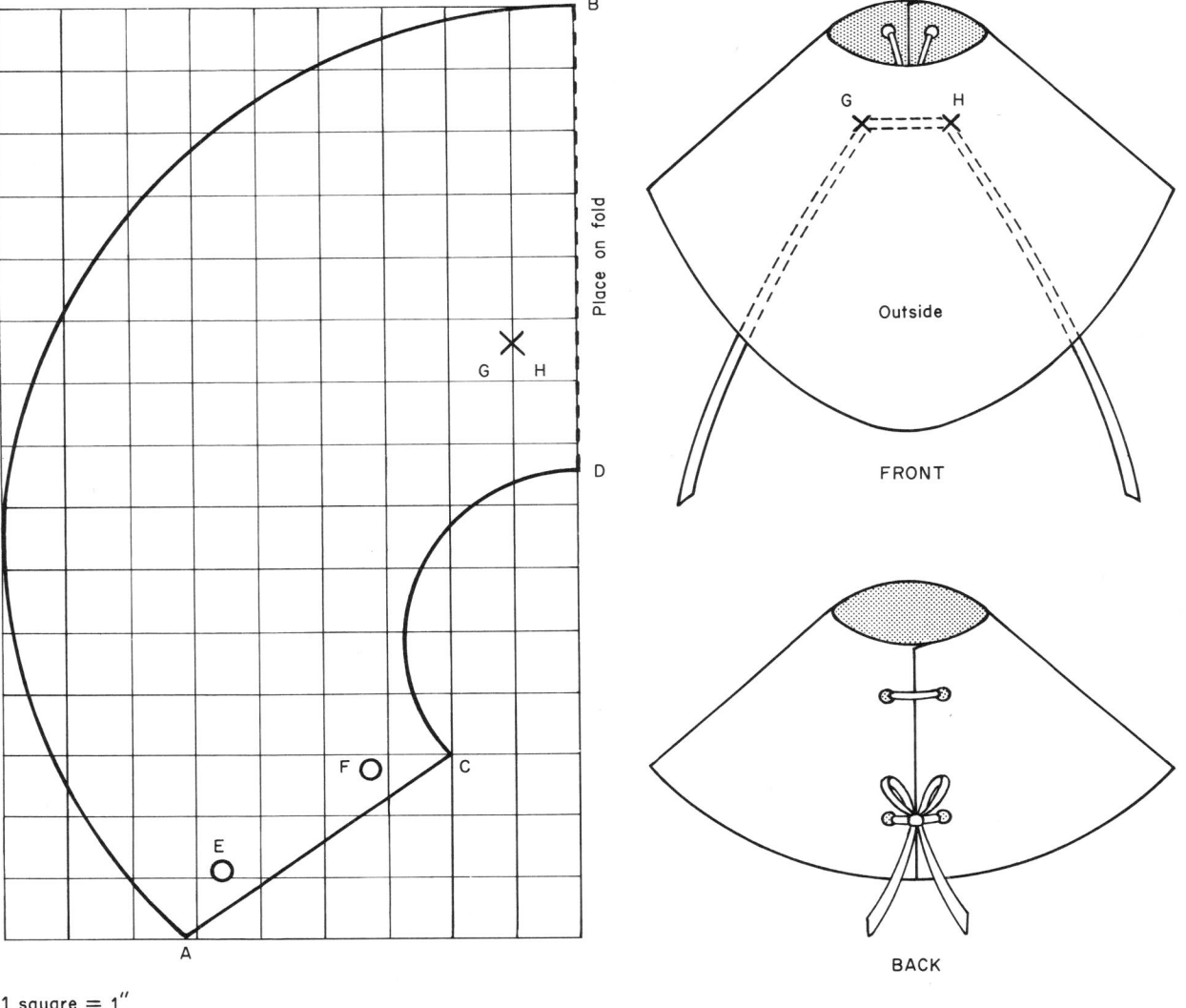

1 square = 1"

Place on fold

B

G H

D

F

E

C

A

Outside

FRONT

BACK

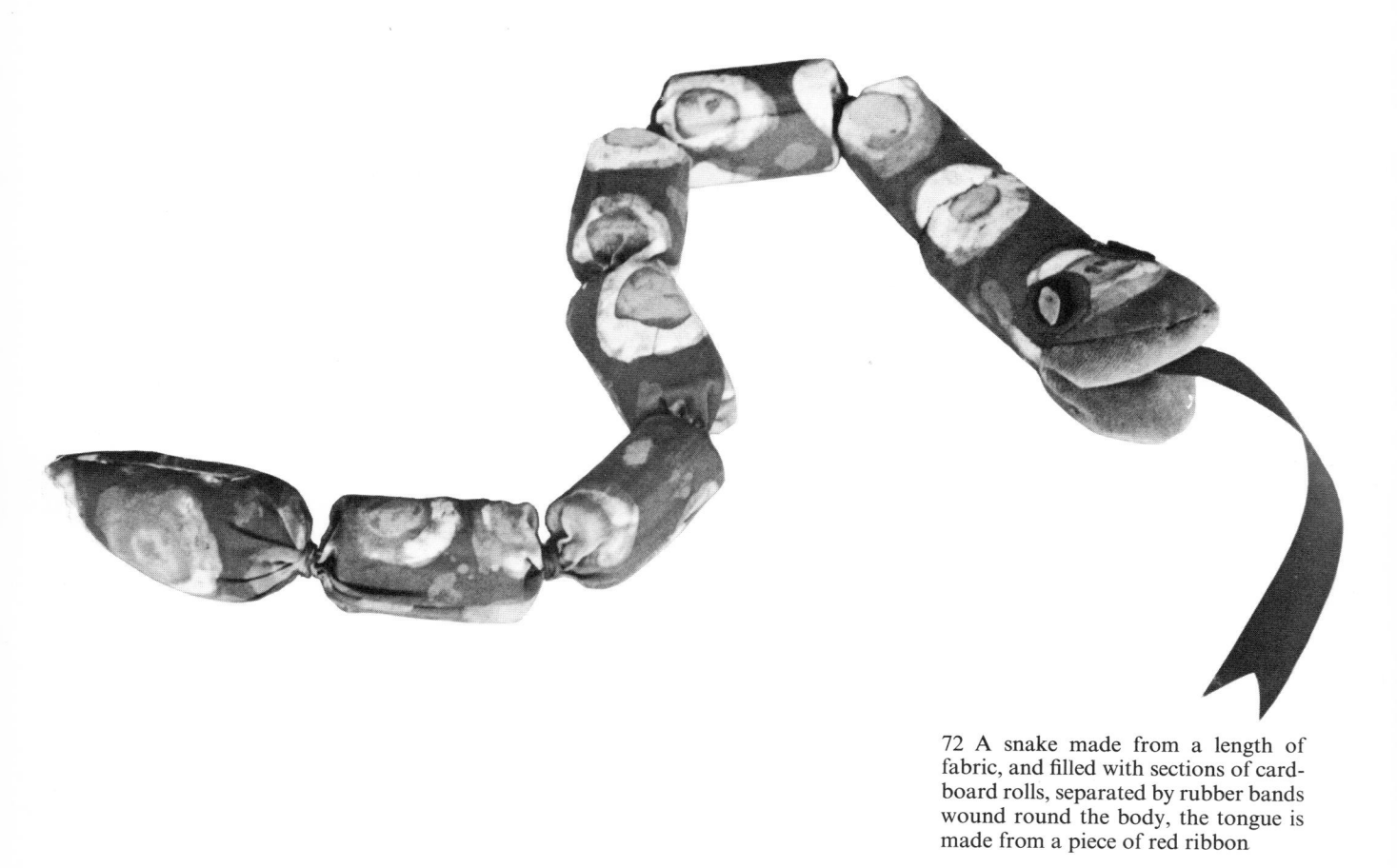

72 A snake made from a length of fabric, and filled with sections of cardboard rolls, separated by rubber bands wound round the body, the tongue is made from a piece of red ribbon

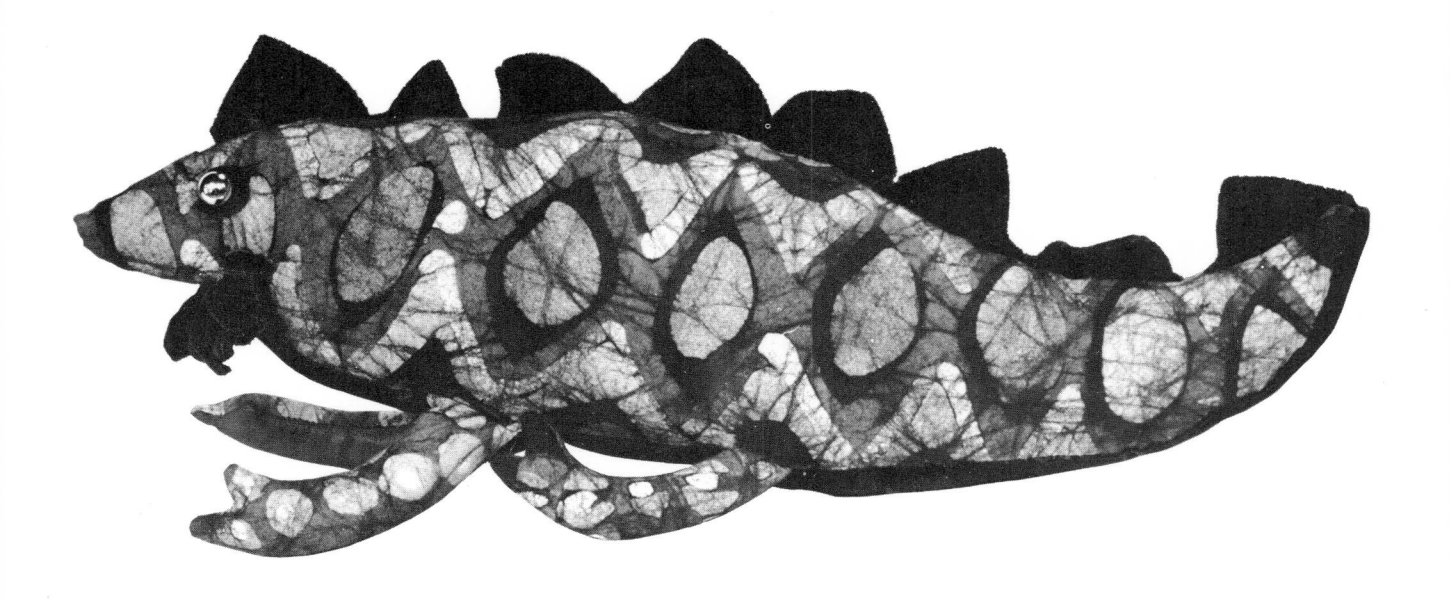

73 A monster dyed in orange, pink and blue and trimmed with purple velvet (Procion)

74 A doll made from experimental scraps from the pattern below

Small pieces of fabrics which are used for experimental purposes make excellent dolls.

Method

Join all four pieces of the body by putting the fabric right sides together, then the foam rubber on the outsides. Sew down each side with a machine, putting a strip of paper under the machine foot to help it to pass over the material easily.

Machine round hands and head.

Stuff the head with cotton wool. Put the head in the neck opening and sew firmly.

Sew short sides of sleeves together. Gather one side, and insert the hands. Turn in once at other edge and sew on the body in the positions marked on the pattern by a dotted line.

Gather the material of oval of base at the edge, insert the cardboard shape.

Turn up once at the bottom of the body, and sew in position.

Put on hair and head dress and decorate as desired.

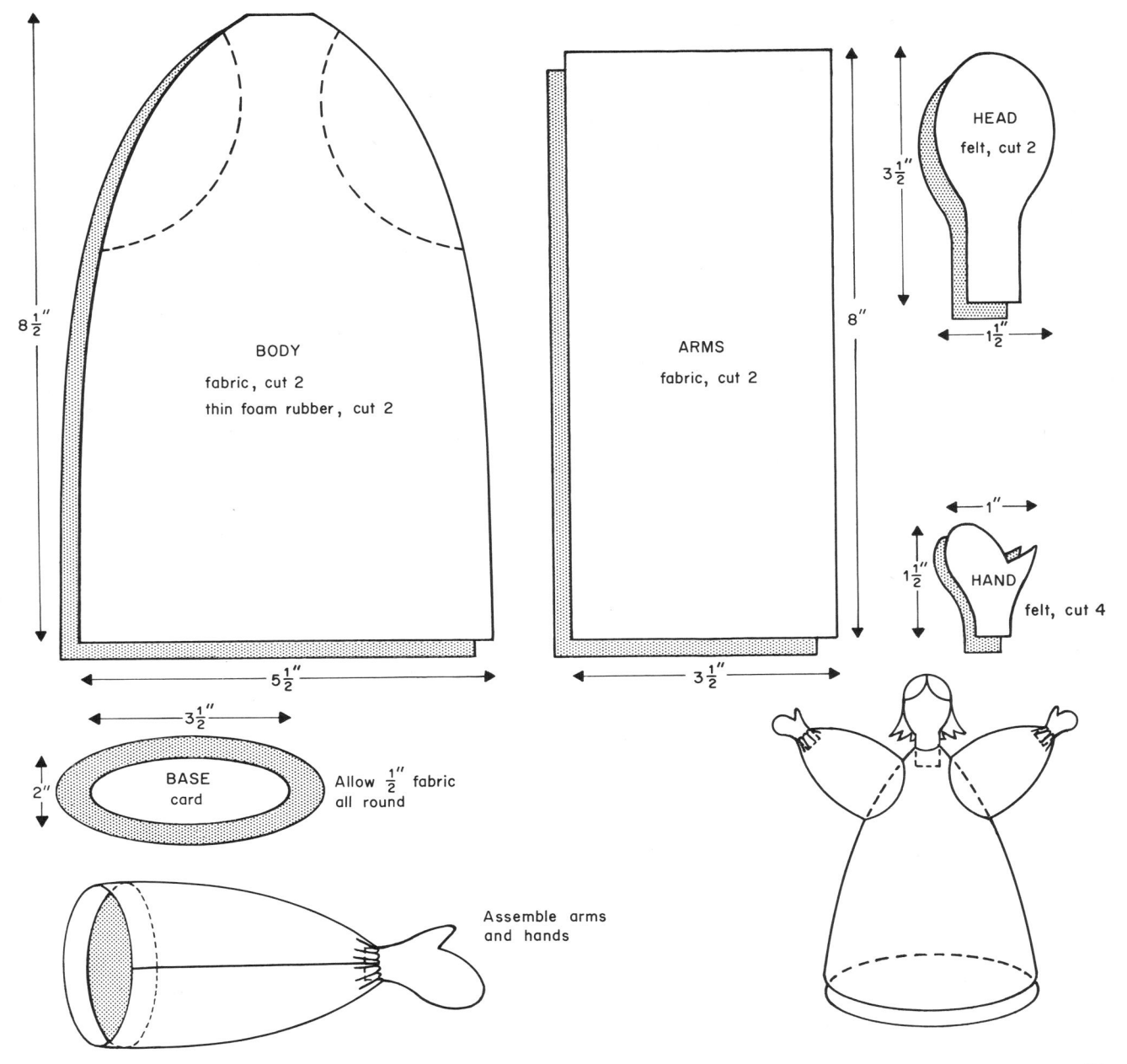

BODY

fabric, cut 2

thin foam rubber, cut 2

$8\frac{1}{2}''$

$5\frac{1}{2}''$

ARMS

fabric, cut 2

$8''$

$3\frac{1}{2}''$

HEAD

felt, cut 2

$3\frac{1}{2}''$

$1\frac{1}{2}''$

$1''$

$1\frac{1}{2}''$

HAND

felt, cut 4

$3\frac{1}{2}''$

$2''$

BASE

card

Allow $\frac{1}{2}''$ fabric
all round

Assemble arms
and hands

75 A picture of a cock in brilliant red Procion dye in different strengths to vary the tone of colour. Finally the fabric was dipped in Procion grey dye for the darkest tone. The wax was painted on with a brush.

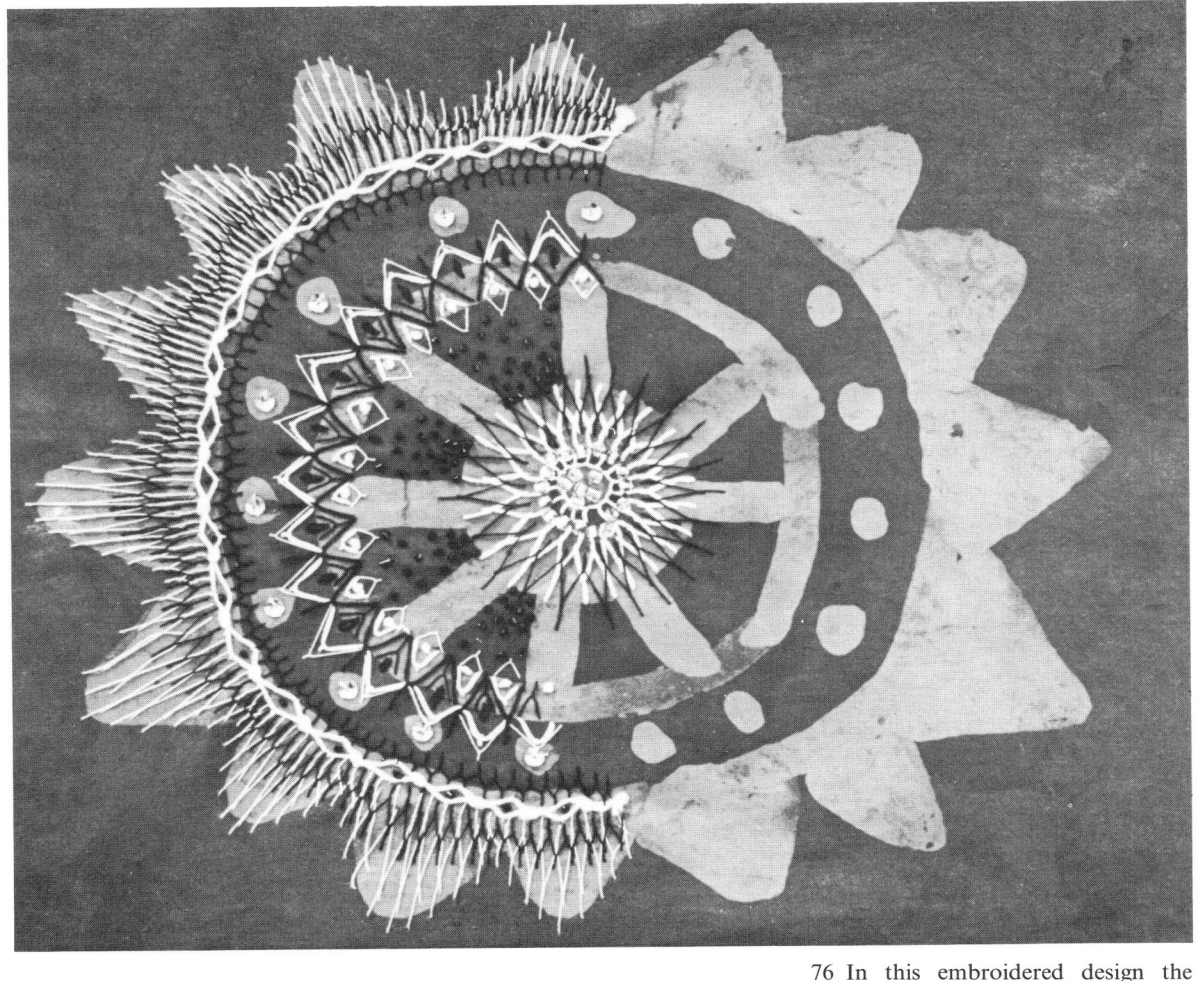

76 In this embroidered design the cloth was dyed brilliant red. Wax was painted on in a wheel shape and the cloth dyed blue. After boiling off the wax the medallion was decorated with beads and simple embroidery stitches in black and white (Procion)

Batik methods are used to make attractive hangings and pictures, building up areas of interesting textures and tones.

The more experienced one becomes with batik methods, the more exciting become the variations and results. It is a craft which gives great satisfaction and can be carried out in the home or school room without large and complicated equipment.

Suppliers in Great Britain

Dyes

Dylon cold water dyes, I.C.I. Procion dyestuff and ancillary chemicals for their application, *Brentamine Fast Black K Salt, Lissapol, Dygon Colour Remover, Urea*

Mayborn Products Ltd
Dylon Works
139–147 Sydenham Road
London E.C.26

Indigo grains and sodium hydrosulphite
Skilbeck Brothers Ltd
Bagnall House
55–57 Glengall Road
London S.E.15

Indigosol dyes, sodium nitrite, beeswax
Dryad Handicraft Ltd
Northgates
Leicester

Manutex
Alginate Industries Ltd
Walter House
Bedford Street
Strand
London W.C.2

Printex (Tinolite) Pigment Colour
Winsor and Newton
Education Division
Wealdstone
Harrow
Middlesex

Commercial urea, potassium permanganate, bicarbonate of soda, calgon
Boots Chemists

Textiles

Emil Adler
46 Mortimer Street
London W.1

Bradley Textiles Co
15 Stott Street
Nelson
Lancashire

Wax trailer or tjanting

Dryad Handicraft Ltd
Northgates
Leicester

D. Mackay
85 East Road
Cambridge

Arts and Crafts Unlimited
49 Shelton Street
London W.C.2.

Slip trailer

E. J. Arnold and Son Ltd
Butterley Street
Leeds 10

Night-lights and calorettes

Price's Candle Distributors Ltd
87 South Lambert Road
London S.W.8

Suppliers in the U.S.A.

Dyes

Craftool Dyes for Batik
Wood-Ridge, New Jersey 07075

Cushing & Co
Dover Foxcroft, Maine 04426

E.I. du Pont de Nemours & Co Inc
50 Page Road
Clifton, New Jersey

Stein, Hall and Co
285 Madison Avenue
New York, N.Y.

Marine Colloids Inc
P.O. Box 70
Springfield, New Jersey 07801

Keltex
Kelco Co
75 Terminal Avenue
Clark, New Jersey

Inko Vat Dye
Screen Process Supplies Manufacturing Co
1199 East 12 Street
Oakland 6, California

Aniline and Aljo batik dyes
Fezandie & Sperrle Inc
103 Lafayette Street
New York, NY 10013

Allied Chemical Corporation
National Aniline Division
40 Rector Street
New York, N.Y.

Synthrapol SP and Procion Dyes M Range
I.C.I. Organics Inc
55 Canal Street
Providence, Rhode Island 02901

Indigisol and Anthrasol Dyes
Carbic-Hoechst Corporation
Sheffield Street
Mountainside, New Jersey

Tinolite Products
Geigy Chemical Company
PO Box 430
Yonkers, New York

Winsor and Newton Inc
555 Winsor Drive
Secaucus, New Jersey 07094

Cassofix FRN-300, fixing agent for direct dyes
Sou-Tex Chemical Co Inc
Mt Holly
North Carolina 28120

Waxes

Norman Ceramics Co Inc
252 Mamaroneck Avenue
Mamaroneck, New York

Craftool Dyes for Batik
Wood-Ridge, New Jersey 07075

Tjanting

Craftool Dyes for Batik
Wood-Ridge, New Jersey 07075

Bibliography

Fabric Printing by Hand, Stephen Russ, Studio London and Watson-Guptill New York

Batik, Nik Krevitsky, Reinhold New York

Textile Printing and Dyeing, Nora Proud, Batsford London and Reinhold New York

Creative Play with Fabrics and Threads, Jean Carter, Batsford London and Watson-Guptill New York

Useful leaflets

Information on Fabric with Indigosol Dyes
Batik Fabrics, J. M. Hobson
obtainable from
Dryad Handicrafts
Northgates
Leicester

Textile Printing and Dyeing with Procion Dyes
This wonderful world of colour

An Introduction to Textile Printing 2nd edition
published by Butterworths in association with I.C.I. Dyestuffs Division
obtainable from
Mayborn Products Ltd
Dylon Works
139–147 Sydenham Road
London E.C.26

Dyes and Dyeing, Pat Gilmour
obtainable from
Society for Education through Art
29 Great James Street
London W.C.1